the

commandments

the net

commandments

how to be a righteous nerd

://norman fraser

Inter-Varsity Press

INTER-VARSITY PRESS
38 De Montfort Street, Leicester LE1 7GP, England
Email: ivp@uccf.org.uk
Website: www.ivpbooks.com

First published 2002

British Library Cataloguing in Publication Data
A catalogue record for this book is available from the British Library.

ISBN 0–85111–258–7

Set in Adobe Garamond 11/13pt
Typeset in Great Britain by Servis Filmsetting Ltd, Manchester
Printed and bound in Great Britain by Cox & Wyman Ltd, Reading, Berkshire

Inter-Varsity Press is the book-publishing division of the Universities and Colleges Christian Fellowship (formerly the Inter-Varsity Fellowship), a student movement linking Christian Unions in universities and colleges throughout Great Britain, and a member movement of the International Fellowship of Evangelical Students. For more information about local and national activities write to UCCF, 38 De Montfort Street, Leicester LE1 7GP, email us at email@uccf.org.uk, or visit the UCCF website at www.uccf.org.uk.

Contents

Preface

Jane was struggling to cope. She was fifteen years old, and the pressures of home and school were piling up for her. When she met James in an online chat room, it was such a relief to be able to open up to someone who cared but was not directly involved. As trust between them grew, the boundaries in their conversations were pushed further and further back. Jane and James started to discuss their most intimate secrets, including their sexual fantasies.

Jane had already run away from home once. When she expressed her dream of running away again, James offered to help her. They agreed to meet.

In fact, 'James' was not one person, but two: James Warren, forty-one, and Beth Loschin, forty-six. As soon as Jane got into their car, she was handcuffed, assaulted and drugged. She was held captive and repeatedly beaten, abused and raped. For two days she was 'lent' to a third person, Michael Montez, with the threat that she would be killed if she did not do whatever he wanted.

Exactly a week after her kidnapping, Jane managed to phone the police, and she was rescued soon afterwards.[1]

It all began with a normal, safe Internet chat session from the privacy of Jane's room. It ended up in unimaginable horror.

This is a book about right and wrong. Its target is not those who perpetrate acts of gross and wilful evil like Jane's violators, but ordinary people like Jane. Jane didn't deserve what happened to her. Of course, she shouldn't have drifted into 'talking dirty' with a strange man in an Internet chat room, but what happened to her was horrific and out of all proportion to her own indiscretions. Nevertheless, her story illustrates how easy it can be for ordinary, 'decent' people like us to drift into behaviours in cyberspace that we would not countenance in normal life. The consequences of such moral lapses can be cataclysmic for the emotional, physical and spiritual well-being of ourselves and others affected by our actions.

It is all too easy to compromise in a rapidly changing world. We convince ourselves we're not sure where the boundaries between right and wrong lie, and whether they too are subject to change. I argue that we would be wise to give careful thought to the way we use computing and communications technology, because failure to think the issues through and to put simple principles of righteous living into practice can lead to untold heartache. This book will not answer all the questions, but my prayer is that it will help you to engage your mind, your heart and your life in the challenge of living righteously for God on the technological frontier. It is offered as a guide, a stimulant, an encouragement and a warning to people who, like me, want to be godly, yet struggle with the practicalities of being good in the contemporary world.

I am grateful to those who have encouraged and helped me during the lengthy gestation of this book. Some have kindly fielded questions I have thrown at them; others have simply shared their love of Scripture and helped me to reflect on faith in action; still others have lent down-to-earth practical assistance. I am happy to record my indebtedness to Wenonah Barton, Jo Bramwell, Tim Chester, John Coffey, Peter Comont, Frank Entwistle, Julian Hardyman, Marcus Honeysett, Bob Horn, Chris Kelly, Mike Kinton, Nigel Lee, John Lennox, Nigel Pollock, Steve Timmis, Tim Vickers, Mark Walton and Tim Wilson. My editor, Stephanie Heald, has always hoped and always persevered with me; it was been a privilege to work with her. Most of all I want to thank my wife, Sarah, for everything.

Norman Fraser

Introduction

nerd /nɜːd//nɜːrd/ *n informal 1 someone who is boring
and unfashionable 2 someone who is extremely
interested in computers.*
(Longman Dictionary of Contemporary English[1])

It was late one night in 1980 that I first became aware of the possibility of 'cybersin'. Though none of us knew it at the time, 1980 was to be an historic year for the future of the human race. IBM had dreamed up the apparently crazy idea of developing a computer so small it could sit on a desk, and so cheap that just about anyone in the West could afford it. During that summer, some IBM executives had dropped in on a tiny Seattle company called Microsoft, run by technology enthusiasts barely out of their teens. The result was a deal for IBM to use Microsoft's operating-system software in their new product: the *personal computer*, or PC.

I knew nothing of this as I sat at a terminal in the university. The PC would not hit the market until the following year, and for the moment I and all the other computer users in my university were forced to compete for access to a central mainframe computer. This vast machine, with its banks of winking lights and busily whirring computer tapes, lived inside a sealed, air-conditioned room, where white-coated operators attended to its needs around the clock.

This great computing dinosaur (it was state-of-the-art technology then) served the whole university, and could support over a hundred simultaneous users scattered around the campus. Because of the way it worked, the more users logged on at any time, the slower everything ran for each user. That's why the real nerds used to work at night, when there were fewer users around.

Once, after a lengthy session of serious work, I had settled down to play with the computer. There were no computer games as we now understand them, but there were plenty of possibilities for amusing oneself – and wasting precious computer time. For all I knew, other users were trying to use the same computer to finish hand-in projects, track astronomical objects, or do vital medical research. It wasn't that I thought these things were unimportant; I just hadn't thought about anyone other than myself.

Suddenly, my screen cleared and then refilled with a stern message, ostensibly from the Chief Computing Officer. My abuse of trust had been noted, it said, and unless I changed my ways, computing rights would be summarily withdrawn.

Ouch! I needed access to the computer for my work. I might as well be ejected from the university as forbidden to use the computer.

In that moment I learned an important lesson: it is possible to do wrong with a computer. In my case, I had acted selfishly by effectively stealing computer time for my own amusement. I had been brought up in a Christian home and was familiar with the idea (and practice!) of sinning with my mind and my body. But here was a new idea: cybersin is a real possibility, and, just like any other variety of sin, it has the capacity to be both fun and dangerous at the same time.

As it turned out, the message on my screen was a hoax. It was the result of someone else's misuse of computer time. But my sense of guilt was real enough. I felt guilty because *I really was guilty*.

New playgrounds for sin

It has always been hard to be good, but in our complex society it seems to be getting harder to recognize where the boundaries lie. For a start, there are so many new contexts in which to sin. And then there are all the new gadgets and technologies to help us sin more efficiently. What is the relationship between technological innovation and Christian conduct? In short, how can we live to please God in the technological society?

The main character in Douglas Coupland's novel *Microserfs*,[2] which follows the fortunes of a group of bright young computer programmers, comes up with this observation:

> 'I got to thinking about sin, or badness, or whatever you want to call it, and I realized that just as there are a limited number of consumer electronics we create as a species, there are also a limited number of sins we can commit, too. So maybe that's why people are so interested in computer "hackers" —because they invented a new sin.'

Have we really invented a new sin after all these years of human wrongdoing? Is 'hacking' a new sin at all, or just a fresh manifestation of one of the old familiar ones?

Let's think about the well-established sin of murder. Murder has always been a possibility for human beings. The Bible recounts how the possibility was turned into grim reality at the earliest opportunity, when Cain killed his brother Abel. It took just one generation of history for murder to appear on the scene.

Now consider what happened to the sin of murder during the Iron Age. New lethal weapons made it easier to turn murderous thoughts into fatal deeds. Millennia later, the invention of the gun further enhanced the ability of people to murder. In each case, the disposition of the human heart to murder was the same, but the advent of technological breakthrough made it easier to turn passions into actions. (This does not imply that technology is by definition bad; after all, it has many positive uses, and weapons can be used in self-defence by the innocent.)

The impact of technological progress on the practice of sin takes several forms, including the following.

First, new technology can make sins easier to commit. As we have seen, improving weapons technology makes murder easier to carry out.

Secondly, new technology can remove obstacles that restrain sin. By removing the fear of unwanted pregnancies, the development of effective contraceptives made fornication and adultery easier in practice.

Thirdly, new technology creates new contexts for sin. Lust is an ancient response of the sinful heart, but the development of technology for portraying first the still and then the moving image facilitated the emergence of pornography as a means of exploring and indulging lust.

Fourthly, new technology furnishes new temptations to commit old sins. Disregard for the property of others is not a new sin, but the advent of spray paint makes it faster and more satisfying to deface property with graffiti.

Finally, new technology magnifies the impact of sin. There used to be a practical limit to how much damage a sociopath could do; nowadays, it could be possible (in theory at least) to wipe out the entire human race using nuclear weapons, germ warfare or chemical pollution.

All this does not imply that technological innovation is wrong in itself, but each innovation forces us to work out how to interact morally with it. As the pace of innovation quickens, so the challenge of keeping at least one step ahead of sin demands increased vigilance.

New technologies are emerging with unprecedented speed, and this is taking place within a wider context of social upheaval; society in the West has undergone dramatic changes over recent years, particularly in the realm of values.[3] Where once there was broad consensus about how to distinguish right from wrong, now there is widespread confusion. Earlier ideas of morality were based on the assumption that values were *given* to all people, rather than constructed by each individual. Specifically, they were given by God, our creator and sustainer. Because he knows us better than we know ourselves, and because he is omnisciently familiar with our universe, he knows what's best for us. More than this, it was believed that God-given morality profoundly reflected aspects of his divine character. He had not arbitrarily stuck labels on behaviours, calling some 'good' and others 'bad'. Rather, what was godly was good, and what was ungodly was bad. Thus, in a theistic society (that is, one in which faith in God is the norm), all values had an absolute basis.

The user manual

It is not the purpose of this book to argue either for the existence of the God of the Bible or for the appropriateness of basing our life and conduct upon him and his self-revelation. These can be explored in detail elsewhere,[4] and supremely in the Bible itself. I shall take them as given and assume a personal Christian commitment on the part of the reader. Without such a commitment, the rest of this book will be difficult to follow, since it concerns practicalities of Christian conduct.

Christians seek to live righteously out of obedience to the Lord, who has already forgiven and accepted us, not out of any belief that good behaviour will somehow buy us access to heaven. How then shall we walk through life as Christians? More particularly, how shall we behave as those who wish to please God when faced with specific situations that Jesus, the disciples and other Bible characters never faced? Take computers: how on earth can we 'walk as Jesus did' (1 John 2:6) when we sit in front of the screen? Jesus never logged on, so how can we take him as our example when we go online?

The Bible tells us that, even though Jesus never used a PC, though he never surfed the Net, played a shoot-'em-up video game or entered an online chat room, he has been tempted in every way, just as we are – yet was without sin (Hebrews 4:15). The surface of things certainly changes – flashy new technologies come along to beguile us – but the human heart remains the same as ever it was. If we look carefully, we shall find things pretty much as they have always been, as the writer of Ecclesiastes asserts:

What has been will be again,
　　what has been done will be done again;
　　there is nothing new under the sun.
Is there anything of which one can say,
　　'Look! This is something new'?
It was here already, long ago;
　　it was here before our time.

(Ecclesiastes 1:9–10)

So if your heart's desire is to follow Jesus and you want to know how to do so in the world of high technology, here's the best possible news for you: God has already given us the answers we need! The answers that worked for previous generations still apply to us and our generation. God has told us what we need to know in the Bible: 'All Scripture is God-breathed and is useful for teaching, rebuking, correcting and training in righteousness, so that God's servant may be *thoroughly equipped for every good work*' (2 Timothy 3:16–17, italics added).

The Bible may be an ancient book, but it remains God's timeless revelation to all people – including us – of how we may find peace with him and live holy lives that please him.

Imagine you've just taken delivery of a complex piece of software. You eagerly install it and try to run the program. Oh dear! There are lots of error messages, and nothing more positive. Eventually, after trying everything you can think of, you call up the customer service hotline for help.

'I assume you followed the installation instructions in the user manual,' the service agent says, with that 'I assume you didn't' tone of voice.

Well, of course you didn't. Who does, these days? But as the conversation progresses you realize that you'd never have got into this mess if you'd just taken the trouble to follow the maker's instructions in the first place. The manual may seem dull by comparison with the program – it may even seem irrelevant – but in truth it is the manual that unlocks the program, making it work to its full potential.

So it is with the Bible, which is the manual God has shipped to users to explain how to get the very best out of human life. Few computer errors are fatal. Systems can be rebooted or the software can be reloaded. But life isn't like that. Some mistakes can be very, very difficult to put right. Sometimes things get broken beyond repair. So we would be fools to ignore the maker's instructions for human life. On the contrary, we ought to be eager to see whether the user manual has any manufacturer's tips on how our lives can be optimized.

For us who believe and trust in Christ, the Bible must not be a dull catalogue of irrelevant rules, but rather a safety lamp for our feet and a guiding light for our path (Psalm 119:105). It should be much more than dead letters on the page as the Holy Spirit himself unfolds Bible truths in our hearts and empowers us to live holy lives that please God (John 14:26; Romans 12:1).

Sometimes, when we try to use an unfamiliar software package without consulting the documentation, we get away with it; our experience or our instincts lead us to the right choices. But only sometimes. Anyone who has worked with computers for any length of time will have encountered the opposite, when experience and instincts lead us to make precisely the wrong decisions.

As in computing, so in life. Our gut feelings and common sense may be invaluable guides in many cases, but they are not infallible. For example, most of us instinctively think of love in terms of emotions. Love is something we feel towards another person. But this is a case where God's manual tells us that our human analysis is incorrect, or, at least, woefully incomplete. True love, it explains, is about deeds more than words or feelings. This can be seen most clearly in Jesus' love for us. He said that he loves us, and that's wonderful, but even more wonderful is the fact that he laid down his life for us, to bring us to God.

It is Jesus' death on the cross that most clearly sums up his love for us. More, it demonstrates the profound love of God the Son for God the Father. In his teaching, Jesus makes it clear that obedience to the Father's wishes is his highest ambition as he seeks to express his love for him. Speaking of his death and resurrection, he said: 'the world must learn that I love the Father and that I do exactly what my Father has commanded me' (John 14:31).

For Jesus, obeying God is a vital part of loving God. And so it must be for us (1 John 5:3).

The quick-start guide

So what are God's commands? The Bible is a long and sometimes difficult book. How can we start to obey God without doing a PhD in Biblical Studies?

Perhaps the best short answer is to be found in the list of instructions for holy living known as the Ten Commandments. These are sometimes caricatured as a stern litany of 'do nots', whose main aim is to banish all fun from life and keep us in a permanent state of repressed gloom.

This could hardly be further from the truth. The Ten Commandments are a gloriously condensed statement of God's good agenda for the human race. They were given in the period of the Old Testament, but they were not superseded by the New (Matthew 5:17). They are not mere tips and hints for how to get on in life, though those who follow them will prosper spiritually. They are not bound by time or culture; after all, they were written on tablets of stone, not in an easily edited word processing file. Even today, thousands of years after God gave them to Moses on Mount Sinai, the Ten Commandments still cry out to be read, pondered and, most of all, obeyed. For they tell us how we may love the Lord our God with all our heart and with all our soul and with all our strength.

The Ten Commandments

1. 'I am the LORD your God, who brought you out of Egypt, out of the land of slavery.
   'You shall have no other gods before me.
2. 'You shall not make for yourself an idol in the form of anything in heaven above or on the earth beneath or in the waters below. You shall not bow down to them or worship them; for I, the LORD your God, am a jealous God, punishing the children for the sin of the parents to the third and fourth generation of those who hate me, but

showing love to a thousand generations of those who love me and keep my commandments.

3. 'You shall not misuse the name of the LORD your God, for the LORD will not hold anyone guiltless who misuses his name.

4. 'Remember the Sabbath day by keeping it holy. Six days you shall labour and do all your work, but the seventh day is a Sabbath to the LORD your God. On it you shall not do any work, neither you, nor your son or daughter, nor your male or female servant, nor your animals, nor the alien within your gates. For in six days the LORD made the heavens and the earth, the sea, and all that is in them, but he rested on the seventh day. Therefore the LORD blessed the Sabbath day and made it holy.

5. 'Honour your father and your mother, so that you may live long in the land the LORD your God is giving you.

6. 'You shall not murder.

7. 'You shall not commit adultery.

8. 'You shall not steal.

9. 'You shall not give false testimony against your neighbour.

10. 'You shall not covet your neighbour's house. You shall not covet your neighbour's wife, or his male or female servant, his ox or donkey, or anything that belongs to your neighbour.'

(Exodus 20:2–17, numerals added)

These divinely ordained commands are timelessly relevant because they reflect God's eternal character and priorities. In the chapters that follow, we shall examine each of the Ten Commandments in turn to see how their ancient teaching can be understood in the context of today's computer and communications technologies. As we proceed, we shall develop a parallel set of commandments, the *Net Commandments*. These are not alternatives to the Mount Sinai originals; rather, they concisely express how the Bible's teaching can be understood in the context of information technologies, and how it can be practically applied to identify cybersin and root it out of our lives.

Righteous nerds

Once upon a time, comparatively few people had access to information technology, and those who did were regarded as a little bit odd. We were the 'nerds', the pasty-faced, square-eyed 'geeks' who were rumoured to be better at communicating with machines than with people. Nowadays, computers are ubiquitous, and everyone has the opportunity to become a nerd. It has even become cool to display nerdy traits openly.

The rise of the computer has lifted cybersin out of the hands of a small techno-priesthood and placed it within reach of everyone.

Newspapers carry a regular stream of headlines bearing on the moral implications of this:

- 'Hard-core pornography freely available on the Internet'
- 'Bank employee diverted electronic money into secret account'
- 'Children hack into military early warning system'
- 'Computer games major cause of time-wasting at work'
- 'Vice ring used Internet to contact victims'

Computer ethics has arrived as a live issue for public discussion. Conscientious Christians need to be aware of the challenges and prepared to use the technology in ways that are good and godly. We may all be nerds nowadays, but let us strive, with the help of God's Word and his Spirit, to be *righteous* nerds.

Prayer

Heavenly Father, you know my strengths and weaknesses; you know the temptations I face and those I have given in to. I confess my tendency to sin in all areas of life.

[Confess and repent of any specific cybersins you know you have committed, so you can receive God's forgiveness and start a new chapter of holy living.]

Please help me as I read this book to learn more from your Word about your purity and holiness, and grant me the wisdom and courage of your Holy Spirit to follow you in the path of holiness.

I ask these things in Jesus' name. Amen.

chapter 1

God first

*'I am the LORD your God, who brought you out of
Egypt, out of the land of slavery.
You shall have no other gods before me.'
(Exodus 20:2–3)*

What happens when we die?

The answer we give to the question of life's ultimate destination will have a significant effect on the way we live now. Or, at least, it ought to. If we believe we will never have to give an account of our actions to an all-seeing God, we may define our own morality according to whatever criteria we choose. If we believe behaviour determines whether we climb upwards or sink downwards in an eternal spiral of reincarnation, we may have an incentive to live a good life, but who's to say what's good and what's not?

Christians believe that we will certainly keep our appointment with God. He's fixed the date and time, and will send transport for us. If we really believe this, it's bound to affect our values and our behaviour.

Few people in history or literature have experienced so crushing a reversal of fortunes as the Old Testament character Job. He lost his family, his business empire and his social standing in a single day, and his health shortly afterwards (Job 1:13–19; 2:7–8). In the midst of all his troubles and woes, it was the prospect of standing before God that kept Job going:

> I know that my Redeemer lives,
>> and that in the end he will stand upon the earth.
> And after my skin has been destroyed,
>> yet in my flesh I will see God;
> I myself will see him
>> with my own eyes – I, and not another.
> How my heart yearns within me!
>
> (Job 19:25–27)

Job saw God as his deliverer, his saviour, and for this reason he longed for the day when he would enter God's presence and see him face to face. Christians share this longing.

We have the privilege of knowing more about our Saviour than Job did, because we live AD rather than BC. The saving love of God for his people has never been so clearly displayed as in the self-sacrificial death of Jesus on the cross for us. If we died with him, we shall also live with him (2 Timothy 2:11). To borrow Job's graphic terminology, after our skin has been destroyed, yet in our flesh we shall see our Redeemer, the Lord Jesus.

Saviour, but not Lord

Perhaps we're happy to have Jesus as our Saviour, but not willing at a practical level to let him be our Lord. We say that Jesus has saved us from judgment, loneliness, spiritual emptiness and despair. We are eager to spend hours singing choruses and being open with other Christians. But giving time to anything that involves pain or hardship is another matter. Perhaps there's nothing in our behaviour to distinguish us from our not-yet-Christian friends, except a thin veneer of pious language. In this way it's very easy for us to reduce the glorious gospel of the risen Lord to a mere personal-fulfillment therapy.

This attitude can be found in all areas of life, including

computer use. The number-one question we ask when deciding whether to hack into someone's files, play video games instead of working or go for a surf in the red-light district of the Internet is no more or less than this: 'Do I feel like it?' And the second question is no loftier: 'Will I be found out?'

Do you see the irony? We claim to follow a Saviour whose central act was the ultimate self-sacrifice. 'That'll do nicely,' we say. 'We'll take the salvation you bought us at such terrible cost, but don't expect us to give anything up or spend our time doing anything distasteful or demanding.'

Guess what? According to Jesus, that's not on. He told his disciples, 'Those who would come after me must deny themselves and take up their cross and follow me. For those who want to save their lives will lose them, but those who lose their lives for me will find them' (Matthew 16:24–25).

These old, familiar words deserve careful consideration. Jesus, the sinless one, identified so radically with us that he took the blame and punishment for our sins on himself at Calvary. To benefit from what he's done, we must follow him to the cross and be radically identified with him.

The apostle Paul explained what this involves: 'We know that our old self was crucified with him so that the body of sin might be done away with, that we should no longer be slaves to sin' (Romans 6:6).

What does that phrase mean: 'that we should no longer be slaves to sin'? Is it reminding us of the fact that Jesus erased our guilt before God and declared us free to enter his presence? Yes, indeed! But it has more to say than that. A few verses further on, Paul continues:

> … count yourselves dead to sin but alive to God in Christ Jesus. Therefore do not let sin reign in your mortal body so that you obey its evil desires. Do not offer the parts of your body to sin, as instruments of wickedness, but rather offer yourselves to God, as those who have been brought from death to life; and offer the parts of your body to him as instruments

of righteousness. For sin shall not be your master, because you are not under law, but under grace (Romans 6:11–14).

We are to take up our cross, not just in the sense of identifying at the moment of our conversion with what Jesus has done once and for all, but daily as we grapple with ongoing temptation to let sin be our master (cf. Luke 9:23). The parts of us that fight against serving the Lord must be put to death; they must be crucified, out of love for him.

Here's the real question to ask when faced with temptation: 'Who or what will be our master? Who will be our Lord?' With our lips we may claim Jesus, but by our lives we may demonstrate a completely different reality.

Faith prompts action

Much of the New Testament is devoted to punching home the truth that we can never earn our salvation by being good. No amount of gold stars or Brownie points will serve to undo the sin that separates us from God. Only simple faith in the atoning work of Christ can bring hope of peace with God.

But that doesn't mean goodness is worthless. Far from it! Real faith in Christ will necessarily lead to changes in behaviour. That's the key Bible idea I want this book to communicate.

No-one makes the point more clearly than James:

> What good is it, my brothers and sisters, if people claim to have faith but have no deeds? Can such faith save them? Suppose a brother or sister is without clothes and daily food. If one of you says to them, 'Go, I wish you well; keep warm and well fed,' but does nothing about their physical needs, what good is it? In the same way, faith by itself, if it is not accompanied by action, is dead.
>
> But someone will say, 'You have faith; I have deeds.'
> Show me your faith without deeds, and I will show you my faith by what I do (James 2:14–18).

Unless our faith actually leads to action – inconvenient, uncomfortable, costly action, like sharing our wealth with an impoverished fellow Christian – then it's all hot air. Just saying you're a Christian doesn't make you one, says James. You've actually got to *be* one.

God's morality

'But I don't know how to be a good Christian!'

Have you ever said these words, or thought them? We know we should be living to please God, but we're not entirely sure what that involves.

The Ten Commandments were given by God to Moses on Mount Sinai to guide the Israelites in all their life and conduct. They laid the foundation for God-centred morality, not just in the Old Testament, but in the New Testament as well, for they are timeless in their scope and concerns.[1]

The First Commandment sets the absolute, non-negotiable ground rule for all dealings with God: 'I am the LORD your God, who brought you out of Egypt, out of the land of slavery. You shall have no other gods before me.' God must be Number One. He is, after all, the ultimate reality. If we don't want to be out of touch with reality, we must allow God to be first in our lives too.

Putting it another way, we must base our lives on the non-negotiable fact of God. He conceived us before there was an 'us' to conceive of him. He brought us into being with a word. When he speaks, the very matter of the universe jumps to do his bidding. He reveals himself to us though we could never have found him. He saves us though we deserve eternal punishment. He is the one before whom we will stand on the Last Day. If there is to be any hope for us as we emerge from death into his presence, it is this: he will recognize us as his willing subjects – those who have been happy to call him 'Lord' and mean it.

Have you noticed how the Lord introduces the Ten Commandments? He doesn't say, 'Go ahead, sinners, make my day! I'm just waiting to zap you as soon as you break one of my commandments.' No, he reminds the people of Israel that he is their proven deliverer, their Saviour, 'who brought you ... out of the land of slavery'. He is already known to them as a loving, caring, compassionate God.

We have a tendency either to live with self-indulgent licence, or to resort to hidebound legalism. Neither extreme is correct. Licence is inappropriate because some things are just plain wrong and must be avoided. The Ten Commandments provide helpful guidance about these. But legalism is inappropriate also. The Commandments are given with a reminder that God hates slavery. A proper understanding of the Ten Commandments must be rooted in the loving character of God. They must not be taken and applied as a system we follow slavishly. They make sense only in the context of a living relationship with our Father in heaven.

Christian morality is not about following dusty rules. It's about living in the light of God's grace and love, and choosing to do what we know he approves because we love him in return.

God must be first, before all else in our lives, not because we have to give way to him, but because we care for no-one and nothing as much as we care for him.

God-free morality

Belief in the God of the Bible used to be widespread in the developed world. This undoubtedly brought some problems, as all established orthodoxies do, but, at bottom, it was rooted in reality. It obeyed the demands of the First Commandment.

Nowadays, God has become an embarrassment to us. Not only have many western people given up faith in a personal God, but they have altogether abandoned a philosophical or religious belief in the existence of truth in any absolute sense. (It appears to matter little to disciples of this worldview that it is based on the nonsensical paradox that the only absolute truth is that there are no absolute truths.) In this context, each person becomes the arbiter of his or her own private morality. How then shall we live with each other as responsible citizens?

In early 1998 *The Sunday Times* published a code of conduct called 'The Ten Commandments Re-written':

1. Be serious
2. Get real
3. Be humble
4. Be quiet
5. Respect age
6. Do not kill, for all murder is suicide
7. Mean what you say
8. Do not steal, or the world will die
9. Honour others; their frailties are usually your own
10. Be kind, be generous and don't sleep around

Each of these 'commandments' seems reasonable, or even positively constructive. But taken together they are nothing short of a scandal, for they promote the disastrous untruth that it is possible to build a coherent moral system without any foundation. In a darkly ironic twist, these politically correct 'commandments' themselves violate the First Commandment. Far from putting God first, they have banished him altogether.

This is not uncommon. People of good intent but no religion have long sought to construct God-free moral codes, such as the following:

- Do to others what you would have them do to you
- Do what you like so long as it doesn't hurt anyone
- Always choose the most loving course
- Pursue the greatest good for the greatest number

Avoidance of selfishness, avoidance of hurt, pursuit of love and happiness: each of these has much to commend it. But on their own they amount to no more than useful rules of thumb. After all, who's to say which is the most loving course when two parties' interests appear to be opposed to each other? When a pregnant woman wants to abort the foetus inside her, shall we show love to the mother or to the child? Shall we calmly accept a situation in which a racist majority declares that it is unhappy with the minorities in its midst and proceeds to persecute them? Or shall we insist that some things are just plain *wrong*, whatever you or I or anyone may think?

The difficulty with principles like these is that they are arbitrary. If love, or avoidance of hurt, or whatever, is to be the basis of our moral system, who says so? Why? Are they just choices plucked out of the air? Or perhaps they are examples of down-to-earth pragmatism: we choose this or that because it seems to work. But what works can be far from obvious. Sometimes it can seem almost more difficult to determine what is the right thing to do than to go ahead and do it.

Upside-down morality

The changing technological climate brings new challenges to those who aspire to live upright lives free from sin. It decrees that absolute values are out and relative values are in. What was once absolutely clear is now only relatively clear. Or relatively unclear. Or something. As if all this were not enough, even our language is changing.

Consider my friend Dave. Dave's eyes widened as I introduced each feature of my new PC to him: the large, high-resolution screen, the only-just-released, top-of-the-range processor, the mind-boggling megabytes of RAM and the gigabytes of hard disk, the ergonomic mouse, the very latest operating system. He was impressed – as any authentic nerd would be. 'Wow!' he whispered, in a reverent ecstasy of technological awe. 'It's really *wicked*!'

In the *Oxford English Dictionary* the word 'wicked' is defined as 'a term of wide application, but always of strong reprobation [i.e. shame], implying a high degree of evil quality'. Is this what Dave meant? No, of course not. What he was trying to convey was that my new PC was truly excellent, even awesome, and I appreciated his sentiments, if not his choice of words.

The recent history of the English word 'wicked' offers an example of what linguists call 'semantic drift', that is, the gradual stretching of a word's meaning to include possibilities far beyond its original scope. Semantic drift can provide us with clues in our language to deeper changes taking place in the attitudes of our society.

Many years ago, in a highly effective National Dairy Council advertising campaign, fresh cream cakes were promoted with the slogan, 'Naughty but nice.' This perfectly captured the feelings of many people when confronted with such a sugary temptation: we know it will do us more harm than good, but we also know it will taste delicious. Many other temptations in life could be described in the same way: naughty but nice. They *feel* nice, but they *are* naughty. The niceness cannot nullify the naughtiness, but it can distract us from it.

But it is possible to become confused and to end up equating naughtiness with niceness; to suppose that unless something's a bit naughty, it can't possibly be nice. Pleasant experiences that lack the *frisson* of broken rules are written off as 'tame' or 'boring'. Their worth becomes related to their capacity to outrage or to challenge convention. The new slogan becomes, 'Nice is necessarily naughty.' Even here, experience shows that there is room for confusion, as prolonged exposure to positively valued 'naughtiness' dulls the conscience and coarsens those involved, leaving them unable to exercise moral discrimination.

And so the word 'wicked', which once could be used to describe only moral depravity and the practice of evil, has drifted to such an extent that it now commonly expresses the exact opposite, namely that which is good and positive.

The same word serves to describe the actions of a Nazi concentration-camp commandant, a paedophile, a petty fraudster, a top athlete, an award-winning actress or a brilliant medical student.

This bewildering range of meanings is captured in recent dictionaries, such as the *Longman Dictionary of Contemporary English*,[2] which lists these three senses for the word 'wicked': '1. Behaving in a way that is morally wrong; evil. 2. *Informal.* Behaving badly in a way that is amusing. 3. *Spoken.* Very good; excellent.'

It's remarkable that we can so easily group together these starkly opposed meanings. It is nothing short of tragic that as humans we have the capacity – and even the tendency – to confuse the underlying realities: to mistake gross moral failure for goodness and real goodness for banality.

If we can't tell the difference between right and wrong,

between good and evil, how can we possibly know how to conduct ourselves as we go through life? We are human beings, but how should we humanly *be*?

The First Commandment lays a sure foundation. God must be first over all. He must be our Lord, whom we obey absolutely. Our obedience should not be mechanical, as if to satisfy the requirements of a moral system; it should be a natural and thankful response to the most amazing fact in the universe: God loves us and we have been granted freedom to live to please him.

Lord of cyberspace

What kind of God shall we follow? Will he be our genie or our Lord? He will be the former if we treat him as a mere spiritual problem-solver. We shall appeal to him when we need help, but feel no sense of obligation to devote our lives to his service.

If we think we can summon him to our aid when we're in distress or when we feel the need of a spiritual dimension in our lives, and then ignore him the rest of the time, we've lost track of which one of us is God in this relationship. That's just about as foolish and dangerous a mistake as it's possible to make.

The First Commandment insists, 'You shall have no other gods before me.' Is there a clause of limitation in there to say that this commandment applies only in certain circumstances? That there are some environments in which it doesn't hold? Of course not. The commandment is expressed in such a way that it has universal application.

This implies that God must be Number One in the world of computer technology, just as in all other spheres. We cannot seriously claim that God is irrelevant or out of his depth in the computer world. He made the silicon that goes into the chips, and the copper that coats the circuit boards. He designed the brains that conceived of computers in the first place, and that write the software now. He made Bill Gates, and he made us, the users. The whole task of science is nothing more than an expedition around the margins of God's handiwork. He knows more than we ever will about information technology, for all information has its origin in him.

But, someone may object, God is the Lord of the *real* world – the world in which it is possible to commit *real* sins. But in *virtual* reality surely it is only possible to commit *virtual* sins?

If we try to argue this, we fail to understand the nature of sin. Though the outworking of sin can be experienced in different ways and environments, it is the source of the sin that counts in God's sight, not the context of its expression. Jesus said: 'What comes out of you is what makes you "unclean". For from within, out of your hearts, come evil thoughts, sexual immorality, theft, murder, adultery, greed, malice, deceit, lewdness, envy, slander, arrogance and folly. All these evils come from inside and make you "unclean"' (Mark 7:20–23).

But surely sins in virtual reality are only imaginary sins?

Notice how many of the sins Jesus listed are primarily sins of the imagination: evil thoughts, greed, malice, envy, arrogance. He will not allow us to dismiss sins of the imagination as inconsequential. Anger will receive the same judgment as murder, and lust as adultery, even though the physical sin is never committed (Matthew 5:21–22, 27–28).

The Bible doesn't give specific, detailed advice about every context in which we human beings may find ourselves. That's because it focuses primarily on the humans rather than the contexts. Sin is a human problem, not an environmental one.

Our task as Christian technology users is to work out what the Bible has to say to us as people first, and then to apply it to ourselves as nerds in a high-tech environment.

The First Commandment is a general stipulation that we must love and serve God before all rivals for our affection and attention. It is not difficult to see how this can be specifically applied in the world of information technology. I've come up with a simple form of words to do this. I call it the First Net Commandment:

The First Net Commandment

Put God first in cyberspace.

There's nothing sacred or prophetic about this wording. It's just an attempt to apply a God-given command from Exodus (20:2–3) to a specific area of life.

Each time you sit down in front of the screen, will you commit to putting God first in cyberspace? The Bible gives us ample grounds for asserting that our God is the Lord of cyberspace. Will he be *your* Lord of cyberspace? Why not take a few moments to commit yourself to this principle? Only when you do can you have any chance of living as a computer user who is righteous in God's sight.

Prayer

Lord God, you know my heart. You know my secret sins. I confess that I have not always put you first in cyberspace. Please forgive my failure to worship you and obey you as Lord in every sphere of life.

I now commit myself to putting you and your glory before all else in cyberspace. I ask for the help and strength of your Holy Spirit to put this commitment into practice and to remain faithful to it.

In Jesus' name. Amen.

chapter 2

God only

> 'You shall not make for yourself an idol in the form of
> anything in heaven above or on the earth beneath or in
> the waters below. You shall not bow down to them or
> worship them; for I, the LORD your God, am a jealous
> God, punishing the children for the sin of the parents to
> the third and fourth generation of those who hate me,
> but showing love to a thousand generations of those who
> love me and keep my commandments.'
> *(Exodus 20:4–6)*

My neighbour was very diligent in his devotions. Each Sunday morning he would rise early and leave the house to go to worship. He would still be engaged in it when we returned from church at lunchtime. Many Christians could have learned a lot from his zeal and commitment, and from the obvious pleasure he took in his worship.

Unfortunately, the object of his veneration was not the Lord God, maker of heaven and earth, but a red Ford Sierra.

A man offering Turtle wax and elbow grease to his car may not be the picture that first springs to mind when the word 'idolatry' is mentioned, but I can think of no other word to describe what I witnessed. My neighbour spent every available moment tending his four-wheeled idol, and, in a strange way, his own sense of confidence and self-worth seemed to be tied up with it. If the car was in good shape, he was in good shape; if the car was a little dusty, he felt personally off colour.

The more usual picture we have of an idol is of a human or part-human form, carved in wood or cast in clay or bronze, sitting in a shrine in a corner of the house, or by the roadside, or in a temple. This is not a common sight in the West. And so we tend to regard idolatry as an obsolete sin. We shrug it off with a simple rationalization – not that the Second Commandment no longer applies, but that idolatry no longer holds any attraction for us and we are no longer vulnerable to its temptations. As far as we are concerned, there might as well be only Nine Commandments, because one of the Ten is irrelevant to us.

If only that were true! If only it were possible for a society to grow out of a sin! Then maybe we might one day grow out of them all and by our own efforts find peace with God. But there can be no such hope. 'The heart is deceitful above all things and beyond cure' (Jeremiah 17:9). The inclination towards idolatry is so deep-seated in the human heart that it cannot be left behind in the onward march of 'progress'. Idolatry is constantly being re-invented in terms that are relevant for each new phase of history. We dare not assume it has been defeated.

Idols in the Old Testament

During their time of slavery in Egypt, the Israelites must have experienced some of the horror of living in a thoroughly idol-atrous society, in which the sun and the moon and various other created things were worshipped, rather than the creator God. He had promised to make the Israelites into a great nation (Genesis 12:1–3), but their bondage in Egypt must have seemed like the victory of idols. (It wasn't: God had foretold in Genesis 15:12–14 that this captivity must come before his promise would be brought to pass.) It's little wonder, then, that prohibitions against idols feature prominently in Scripture in the period immediately following the escape from Egypt.

The first command God gave on Mount Sinai was that he must come first for the Israelites (Exodus 20:3). The second was that he must have no rivals at all – not even subsidiary ones. There must be no idols. God first. God only.

Failure to comply with the Second Commandment would be judged severely. Idolatry is not just a private sin; it is a terrible public wrong, poisoning a society in ways that can take generations to heal (Exodus 20:4–6).

The ingrained nature of idolatry was starkly demonstrated on the day Moses descended from Mount Sinai, where God had been giving him the Ten Commandments. It must have been the crowning experience of Moses' life to spend so much time in the presence of the Lord, and to be shown a glimpse of his plans and purposes. But the glory of basking in God's company was rudely interrupted by an unwelcome report from the Israelite camp in the plain below. 'The LORD said to Moses, "Go down, because your people, whom you brought out of Egypt, have become corrupt. They have been quick to turn away from what I commanded them and have made themselves an idol cast in the shape of a calf"' (Exodus 32:7–8).

Imagine you are being interviewed for a job as a head teacher. You have just finished explaining your tough approach to school discipline when the Chairman of School Governors receives an SMS message. He looks at you and says, 'It seems we need proceed no further; your son has just burnt the school to the ground. I think you've probably got business to attend to elsewhere. Good day.'

Moses must have felt a bit like that. As he hurried to break up the idolatrous orgy at the bottom of the mountain, he threw down the stone tablets on which God had written the Commandments, breaking them into pieces (Exodus 32:19). Though it was an act of anger or frustration, in a way it was also prophetic, for the Israelites would shatter the Ten Commandments over and over again, not least through their persistent return to idolatry.

The folly of idolatry is a favourite theme of the Old Testament prophets. The idea that something we have made with our own hands should be worthy of our worship is so foolish that the prophets don't so much argue against it as pour scorn on it. It is an absurd idea – so ridiculous that to take it seriously would be to accord it more dignity than it deserves. Isaiah (44:13–20) describes a man who chops down some wood. Some he uses for cooking and heating.

> From the rest he makes a god, his idol;
>   he bows down to it and worships.
> He prays to it and says,
>   'Save me; you are my god.'

(verse 17)

According to Isaiah, you've got to be a blockhead to worship a block of wood. It is the consistent refrain of the Old Testament that idols are no more than low-grade frauds perpetrated by the cynical on the credulous, or, worse still, by fools on themselves (Jeremiah 10:14–15).

Idols in the New Testament
In the New Testament, the idea of the idol as representative of a greater reality is more clearly developed. This can be seen in the case of Artemis.

The Greek goddess Artemis (equivalent to the Roman Diana) was the goddess of the moon and of hunting, and a fertility cult was associated with her worship. The temple of Artemis at Ephesus was one of the Seven Wonders of the Ancient World. It had a great, high chamber, supported by a hundred vast columns, containing as its centrepiece a statue of the goddess. This was said to have fallen from the sky (Acts 19:35), and was the focus for Artemis worship.

Around the temple a thriving industry churned out miniature replicas of the idol and shrines for the faithful to take home. When Paul arrived in Ephesus with his message of one true God, who rejects idols, the Ephesus Guild of Idolmakers saw trouble on the horizon. Their businesses were threatened. Their resistance was organized by a silversmith called Demetrius. Paul, he complained, 'says that gods made by human hands are no gods at all. There is danger not only that our trade will lose its good name, but also that the temple of the great goddess Artemis will be discredited, and the goddess herself … will be robbed of her divine majesty' (Acts 19:25–27).

The meeting between faith in the one true God and faith in false gods and their idols cannot be cordial. The latter can be robbed of their 'divine majesty' if people stop worshipping them. By contrast, the Lord God's divinity is inherent in his nature, and all things proceed from him, even life itself. 'Therefore, since we are God's offspring,' Paul proclaimed on another occasion, 'we should not think that the divine being is like gold or silver or stone – an image made by human design and skill' (Acts 17:29).

God is the very source of life. Faith in Christ is living faith in a living God. Christianity does not depend on visible objects; it depends on the Lord Jesus, who is made known to us by the Holy Spirit, who lives in our hearts. 'For we are the temple of the living God' (2 Corinthians 6:16).

In the area of worship, the heart of the matter is the human heart. Idolatry doesn't emanate from bronze or silver or wood statuettes; it emanates from hearts that designate these otherwise worthless objects worthy of worship. Ephesus may be famous for the great idol of Artemis inside the renowned temple, but less well known is the fact that the temple of the human heart is stuffed full of idols, and these are more subtle and insidious because they cannot be directly seen.

In his letter to Christians at Ephesus, Paul defines an 'idolater' as an 'immoral, impure or greedy person' (Ephesians 5:5). Immorality, impurity, greed – these are idols of the heart. So are lust and evil desires (Colossians 3:5). 'Ultimately, any violation of God's law is idolatry, and idols may serve as an image and label for all that is anti-Christian (1 John 5:21).'[1] 'The idol is whatever claims that loyalty which belongs to God alone (Isaiah 42:8).'[2]

Computers as idols

'There's a one-eyed yellow idol to the north of Khatmandu', runs the poem of Milton Hayes.[3] Is it possible that our winking, green-eyed computer has become our idol?

In a superficial way the PC is a bit like a god in a shrine. It sits on its own special desk, surrounded by its accessories. It requires to be placated with fresh supplies of electricity and occasionally to be fed with a new disk. We go to it for answers to some of the difficult questions of life, and sometimes we just go to relax in its presence. We may consider it cleverer than ourselves, or more powerful. And so we respect it, and treat it with a certain reverence.

It's easy to overstate the similarities. If the heart of idolatry is the human heart rather than the external object of veneration, the real test of whether our computers have become idols is whether they 'claim that loyalty which belongs to God alone'.

The Dutch politician and economist Bob Goudzwaard has written about the reality of idolatry in western society:

> ... gods never leave their makers alone. Because people put themselves in a position of dependence on their gods, invariably the moment comes when those things or forces gain the upper hand ... It is conceivable then that the means to progress which our own hands have made – the economy, technology, science and the state – have become such forces today, imposing their will on us as gods.[4]

One of the key features of idolatry Goudzwaard identifies here is the placing of ultimate trust in the idol. Instead of saying, 'We know things will turn out to be all right because of the unfailing love of God', it is tempting to think, 'Our idols will protect us.'

Another feature of idolatry is the surrendering of initiative. Where once we used our own judgment, now we surrender to the 'logic' of the idol. In the case of technology, this means that 'progress' becomes its own justification, its own morality:

> Convincing themselves that what technology *can* do it *must* do, some may demand that we adapt indiscriminately to the requirements of modern technology. To

them unrestricted technology offers a better life, more luxury, more prosperity and better health, not to mention solutions to a number of current world problems. Others may entrust to unhampered technological development their deepest security needs, believing that superior weapons technology insulates them from the hands of any possible enemy. To these persons and nations technology has become an idol.[5]

A further feature of idolatry is fear:

We all know that fear plays an important role in idolatry. Fear arises because gradually the roles of idol and idol worshipper undergo a reversal. First, people make an idol. They fashion an image however they wish. Soon, however, they become dependent on their own creation. No wonder: having given the creation its own life, it has a grip on them. The slightest misstep can trigger the wrath of the idol, a wrath which may even bring them to ruin.[6]

Many people are afraid of computers because they don't understand them. They stand in awe of the raw power of calculation and the speed of operation. Others have placed such confidence in computers that they have allowed activities that used to include human checks and balances to be fully automated in a way that is simply foolish.

The human relationship with idols has always combined love and hate, adoration and fear. For every person who sees computers as frightening and dangerous, it is possible to find another who sees them as our best hope for the future.

The Greek god Theuth was said to be an inventor, with a host of brilliant discoveries to his credit, including numbers, calculation, geometry, astronomy and writing. According to Socrates, he was also a tireless advocate of new ideas. The communications theorist Neil Postman sees some of the same enthusiasm in our own society:

We are currently surrounded by throngs of zealous Theuths, one-eyed prophets who see only what new technologies can do and are incapable of imagining what they will *undo*. We might call such people Technophiles. They gaze on technology as a lover does on his beloved, seeing it as without blemish and entertaining no apprehension for the future. They are dangerous and are to be approached cautiously.[7]

Technophiles don't just like technology; they confess their need of a saviour and think technology offers the best candidate(s). Postman speaks of the 'god of Technology'. It is a god

... in the sense that people believe technology works, that they rely on it, that it makes promises, that they are bereft when denied access to it, that they are delighted when they are in its presence, that for most people it works in mysterious ways, that they condemn people who speak against it, that they stand in awe of it, and that, in the born-again mode, they will alter their lifestyles, their schedules, their habits, and their relationships to accommodate it.[8]

This quasi-religious faith in technology is sometimes called 'technism':

Technism reduces all things to the technical; it sees technology as the solution to all human problems and needs. Technology is a saviour, the means to make progress and gain mastery over modern, secularised cultural desires ... Technism constitutes a new faith, a new religion.[9]

If technism is a new faith, the computer is its highest deity. This doctrine is spelt out unambiguously by Robert Jastrow, a theoretical physicist who played an important role in planning the scientific exploration of the moon:

> The era of carbon-chemistry life is drawing to a close on earth and a new era of silicon-based life – indestructible, immortal, infinitely expandable – is beginning … The computer – a new form of life dedicated to pure thought – will be taken care of by its human partners, who will minister to man's social and economic needs. It will become his salvation in a world of crushing complexity.[10]

The computer is certainly a useful tool for solving social and economic problems. But 'our salvation in a world of crushing complexity'? I think not. A line has been crossed, and justifiable appreciation of computers has turned into old-fashioned idolatry.

Technoshamanism, technopaganism and extropianism

A fundamental difference between believers in God and atheists is how they understand consciousness. Theists believe consciousness to be basic, and the material world secondary. The foundation of all things is the infinite, transcendent consciousness we call God. 'In the beginning was the Word' (John 1:1). 'And God said, "Let there be …"' (Genesis 1:3). Atheists, by contrast, regard matter as basic and consciousness as secondary, a fascinating phenomenon emerging by happy accident out of the physics of brains.

New Age thinkers are highly secularized in attitudes and lifestyle, but they are dissatisfied with materialism's secondary view of consciousness and dismissal of all things spiritual. Unlike biblical theists, they believe in an impersonal 'cosmic consciousness', of which they consider their own consciousness to be part.

Douglas Groothuis has been one of the most trenchant Christian critics of the New Age.[11] He writes:

> The yearning for a New Age to spring from the divine depths of human consciousness is hardly new; it is an ancient aspiration, an occult orientation to the divine, the world and the self that sees them all as part of one ultimate reality. The new spin on the old view is the

addition of cybertechnologies as essential aids in the process of self-discovery or even as the manifestation of the New Age itself ...

A raft of technopagans are tapping into cyberspace as a realm for mystical discovery, magical powers, and evolutionary enhancement. The use of cyberspace for these ends is called technoshamanism ... Although it is not an organized movement, it represents a growing cultural trend to deify cyberspace. The tribal shaman of ancient, pagan religions was a mediator between spiritual and material worlds who experienced mystical ecstasies and initiated others into the same communion with higher powers. Technoshamanism eliminates the middleman – although it is not without visionaries, philosophers, and programmers – and offers mystical connections in cyberspace to everyone with a modem.[12]

Technoshamanism is very much in the spirit of idolatry. The problem is not with cyberspace *per se*, or with the technologies that support it. Rather, the problem is with the user who engages with a thing – even an abstract thing like cyberspace – and ascribes to it some of the attributes or obligations due to God. Rightly viewed, cyberspace is an ingenious human invention; wrongly viewed, it becomes an idol.

New technological spiritualities are evolving all the time. One that is still in a fairly early stage of development, but is likely to grow in years to come, is *extropianism*. This is the belief that it will one day be possible to download all one's memories, characteristics, personality – in short, one's essential self – from the brain into some alternative storage device, such as a hard disk or silicon chip. This would effectively separate 'me' from my body, and thus liberate me to live past my body's physical death. Dr Bart Kosko, no fringe New Age guru, but a respected mathematician from the University of Southern California, explains:

> You go to sleep one night and wake up in a chip. Your brain switches from meat to silicon but you are the

same. At least at first you are. The old memories are still there but now you do not access them the same way. They are not just vivid when you recall them. They are as intense as when you first lived them. And you can edit them as if they were dreams you controlled. Your memory is just one small database that you can access at the speed of light. You can sense all stored knowledge of art and science and news and history much as you can now scan a newspaper. And you can feel and act and do it alone or with thousands of other chip souls.[13]

It is the vision of uniting all downloaded subjective consciousnesses into a single, grand, unified 'collective consciousness', along with all available objective information, that really excites extropians. For then we would, collectively, be both immortal and omniscient. We would have become like God. Kosko continues:

Religion holds no monopoly on the concept of heaven … Heaven in a chip completes the rival world view of science. The Creation myth gives way to the Big Bang … Divine law gives way to the laws of math and science. The soul gives way to complex information processing. The Resurrection gives way to cryonics and cell repair with nanocomputers or to the gentle sleep that takes you from brain to chip.

Biology is not destiny. It was never more than tendency. It was just nature's first quick and dirty way to compute with meat. Chips are destiny.[14]

I have personally met some distinguished scientists who are convinced extropians. Not only do they long for the state of affairs described by Kosko, but they confidently expect to see at least the first steps towards it during their lifetime.

There are two profound problems with their stance. First, they assume that persons are no more than the sum of the content of their brains. Christians differ in the way they under-stand the traditional parts of a person (spirit, soul and body), but they all agree that to bear God's image is to be more than just a set of neural states in a brain. Who knows? It may turn out to be possible to download certain attributes of my cognitive make-up into a chip, but that will not be – and never could be – the same as downloading the unique 'me', who was known by God before the foundation of the world (Psalm 139:13–16; Jeremiah 1:5).

The second, and more serious, problem with extropianism is that it sets its face resolutely against God. It commits precisely the technological idolatry of the builders of the Tower of Babel, who thought that with bricks and bitumen – the works of their hands – they could reach up to heaven (Genesis 11:1–9). The very thought is blasphemous. But then, the same can be said of idolatry in all its forms.

Idols with keyboards

> The real enemy of true knowledge of God is not atheism … The real enemy is rival gods, and the defin-ing challenge is 'Choose for yourselves this day whom you will serve' (Joshua 24:15).[15]

God made us in his own image (Genesis 1:26–27). This is not to say that people – with one head, two arms, two legs and a navel – look like God. Indeed, visual descriptions of God are noticeable by their absence from the Bible. Even the hints we do find clearly serve a symbolic function (for example, Genesis 15:12–21; Isaiah 6:1–5; Ezekiel 1; Daniel 10:4–6; Acts 9:3–5; Revelation 19:11–16).

God made us in his own image in a more profound way, and we long to be like him. We long to be good and pure and lovely and righteous, for the lack of these qualities is a heavy burden to bear. It is right for us to yearn for godliness (1 Timothy 4:8; 6:11). But there is a kind of longing to be like God that is pure blasphemy: the longing for power, self-determination and the worship of others. This was the weakness the serpent in the

Garden of Eden played to when he said to Eve, 'when you eat of [the fruit] your eyes will be opened, and you will be like God' (Genesis 3:5).

Idolatry is born out of our desire to be like God. It begins with people creating in their own image, as God did. Primitive cultures create physical replicas of human beings. In more complex cultures the visual qualities of the idol are less significant, and other aspects of our human image begin to dominate.

The idolizing of computer technology is a particularly potent form of idolatry, for it doesn't rely on the appearance of the computer. Indeed, the physical computer may never be seen. But the computer is none the less created in our image, and especially in the image of our rationality.[16]

But we are not God, and we fool ourselves if we think we could be. For God has made us to glorify and enjoy *him* for ever.[17] When we make an artefact in our own image, the natural inclination of our sinful hearts is to glorify and enjoy *it*. God made us to worship *him*; we make idols so we can worship *them*. It is the ultimate folly.

The dimensions of the universe are beyond our comprehension, but there is room for only one God. It's like in marriage, where there is room for just one husband and one wife. Reasonable people will be delighted if their spouse has many friends, but ferociously jealous if he or she takes another lover. So in the Second Commandment the Lord God uses the language of marriage[18] to explain that he will not tolerate rival gods: 'I, the LORD your God, am a jealous God' (Exodus 20:5).

It's not wrong to find computers useful. It's not wrong to be keen on computers. But it's wholly unacceptable for enthusiasm for computers to eclipse enthusiasm for the Lord God. It's wrong for confidence in computers to be greater than confidence in God. And it's wrong for fear of computers to be greater than reverent fear of the one who is truly to be feared: the Lord God Almighty (Deuteronomy 4:23–24; Luke 12:5). These things are idolatrous, and must be renounced if the one who, above all else, is faithful and true (Revelation 19:11) is to reign as Lord in our lives.

Determine today to live by the Second Net Commandment:

The Second Net Commandment

Do not allow technology to become an idol.

Prayer

Lord, you are the one true God, ruler of heaven and earth, Lord of all. I confess there have been times and ways I have allowed other things to take your place in my life – the place that is rightfully yours, and yours alone.

[Confess any specific instances of idolatry in your life.]

Forgive me these sins, I pray, and others like them that I don't even realize or remember. Give me the strength, Lord, to turn from them and worship you alone. Help me not to allow technology to become an idol. I commit myself to worshipping you alone as Lord and God. Please help me to keep your commandments, and show your love to me.

In Jesus' name. Amen.

chapter 3

God's name

*'You shall not misuse the name of the LORD your God,
for the LORD will not hold anyone guiltless who misuses
his name.'*
(Exodus 20:7)

'Norman' is probably not the name I would have chosen for myself. In TV comedies you can usually guess that a character is called Norman before you hear his name; he's the clown, the buffoon, the village idiot.

Once, as a student, I was travelling on a train when my companion spotted the name of the station we were passing through, and started to laugh. When I asked what was so funny, he pointed to the station sign.

'I didn't realize there was such a place in real life. I always thought it was just a "joke name" that had been made up by comedians to sound funny.'

After he'd recovered enough to wipe the tears from his eyes he added a further confession: 'To be honest, I always thought "Norman" was just a joke name until I met you!'

I don't hate the name, though. I don't feel personally insulted when I hear an ultra-nerdy person being described as 'a bit of a

Norman'. And I can laugh with everyone else when I hear a good Norman joke.

'Sticks and stones may break my bones but names can never hurt me.' So runs the old children's defence against playground insults, and it's true that some kinds of playful or even malicious name-calling have no real effect on us. But people can be deeply hurt by name-calling. As Christian believers we need to understand that even God has sensitivities in this area.

The Third Commandment warns us against misusing the name of the LORD, and solemnly promises that 'the LORD will not hold anyone guiltless who misuses his name'. It vital for us to understand what it means to misuse the Lord's name.

Naming names

In one sense, names are just labels by which objects may be known. For example, there is nothing about the word *black* that makes it inherently more suitable as a label for what it describes than any other word. If all the speakers of English in the world decided at midnight today to reverse the meanings of the words *black* and *white*, communication would not suffer. We would talk about the night being *pitch white*, and clean shirts being *brilliant black*. So long as everyone agreed on the new convention, we would get along happily enough.

Words are arbitrary labels for entities in the world. That's why Adam, rather than God, is pictured in the Bible at the beginning of human history, getting on with the task of naming: '… whatever the man called each living creature, that was its name. So the man gave names to all the livestock, the birds of the air and all the beasts of the field' (Genesis 2:19–20).

The arbitrariness of names extends even to the name of God himself. He may be eternally unchangeable, but there is nothing divinely fixed about the word 'God'. The same almighty divinity may be known as *God* in English, *Bog* in Russian and *Dio* in Esperanto, but these are just names. It is the Lord who gives the names their meaning, not the names that make him who he is.

Of course, there's more to names than this, for once a name has been coined, it can be used to stand in place of the person it

names. My name written by my own hand on a cheque is suffi-
cient to persuade my bank to pay bills on my behalf. It is not
necessary for me to visit the bank to make this happen; it is
enough for my name to serve in my absence.

This principle applies when we pray. If we come to God and
present requests to him in prayer, he may rightly ask why he
should pay any attention to us. After all, he is holy and awesome
and we are habitual sinners. The reason God *does* listen to us
and take our prayers seriously is that we present them to him in
the name of Jesus, the spotless one, the Father's only begotten
Son. Jesus himself taught us to do this: 'I tell you the truth, my
Father will give you whatever you ask in my name. Until now
you have not asked for anything in my name. Ask and you will
receive, and your joy will be complete' (John 16:23–24).

Jesus has given us authority to use his name. It is as if he has
given us his own Bank of Heaven credit card and told us to spend
as much as we need; the bill will be charged to his account. The
analogy is not perfect, but it conveys something of the astonishing privilege of being able to pray in the name of Jesus. We
receive what Jesus deserves because we pray in his name, with his
authority.

Where the credit-card analogy needs to be handled with care is
in respect of the relational aspect of prayer. It would be wrong to
abuse the trust of a parent who has given us a credit card against
his or her bank account. So also it would be wrong to pray self-
indulgently without regard for the one in whose name we pray.
He is the one who has to 'foot the bill' of our prayers.

'Lord, won't you buy me a Mercedes Benz?' runs the refrain of
the song made famous by Janis Joplin.[1] But is this the kind of
prayer Jesus wants to underwrite with his name? Of course not!
He gives us his name so that we can do his will – so that we can
carry out the good works he has prepared in advance for us to do
(Ephesians 2:10). Our requests must be 'according to his will' (1
John 5:14), and thus modelled on the attitude of Jesus himself:
'not as I will, but as you will' (Matthew 26:39). To help us understand what God's will is, the Father has given us his Holy Spirit,
in the name of the Son (John 14:26). In this way, our prayers can

be the kind to which Jesus will gladly say 'Amen' at the right hand of the Father in Heaven.

Word magic

In many cultures, the connection between words and things is believed to be so close that merely uttering the right words can change reality. This is the basis of much primitive magic, in which spoken spells and incantations are assumed to have power to alter events in the physical world. This is how curses are supposed to work: bad words spoken against a person are intended to cause bad things to happen to that person.

Word magic is based on the belief that some words have power in themselves. In the story of Ali Baba and the Forty Thieves, the only way to gain access to the cave of the forty thieves was to utter the magic words, 'Open, Sesame!'

It's important to understand that the power of the name of Jesus, used in prayer, has nothing to do with word magic. Using the name of Jesus is not at all like 'Open, Sesame!' Rather, it confesses that we are acting in obedience to the commands of Jesus, and asking the Father to show mercy for the sake of Jesus and what he accomplished on the cross in reconciling us to God.

You can't separate the name of Jesus from the person of Jesus.

This truth is graphically demonstrated in the story of the seven sons of Sceva, who tried to use the name of Jesus as a magic word, and quickly came to regret it.

> Some Jews who went around driving out evil spirits tried to invoke the name of the Lord Jesus over those who were demon-possessed. They would say, 'In the name of Jesus, whom Paul preaches, I command you to come out.' Seven sons of Sceva, a Jewish chief priest, were doing this. One day, the evil spirit answered them, 'Jesus I know, and I know about Paul, but who are you?' Then the man who had the evil spirit jumped on them and overpowered them all. He gave them such a beating that they ran out of the house naked and bleeding (Acts 19:13–16).

The sons of Sceva had either witnessed or heard of Paul performing miracles in the name of Jesus. But they didn't know Jesus themselves, so their invoking of his name had no reality behind it. They paid for their presumption with a beating. This acted as a scary warning for those who heard news of it: '... they were all seized with fear, and the name of the Lord Jesus was held in high honour' (Acts 19:17).

It's interesting that people didn't say, 'Well, I don't think much of this new magic word "Jesus". It didn't work for the sons of Sceva.' No, they correctly realized that here was a personal source of power far beyond their own, and one whose name should not be treated lightly. And so the name of the Lord Jesus came to be held in high honour.

Honouring the name of the Lord

One of the chief ways in which the name of the Lord can be honoured is by refusing to separate it from the person of the Lord. This may sound rather complex and theological, but it's really quite straightforward.

If you forge my signature in my cheque book, you are invoking my name without involving my person. If you pretend I said something I didn't really say, you are invoking my name without involving my person. If you tell a lie about me, you are invoking my name without involving my person. In each case, not only do you cheat other people, but you dishonour me.

If we want to honour the Lord, we must be careful to invoke his name only when we mean to involve his person.

We honour Jesus when we pray in his name because he pleads our case at the right hand of our Father in heaven. We honour the Father when we take care to listen to his words, and when we pass them on to others accurately. We honour our God when our words and our lives tell the truth about who he is.

In short, we honour the Lord when we honour the name of the Lord. And we honour his name when we use it seriously and reverently to tell the truth about him, not frivolously or carelessly to amuse ourselves.

Perhaps the most obvious way in which the Lord's name is

used frivolously is in swearing. 'Jesus Christ!' people may gasp when they really mean 'Oh!' or 'Wow!' They may use 'God' as no more than a kind of audible punctuation. Or they may ask someone to do something 'for God's sake', when what they really mean is that they want it done for their own sake.

This kind of misuse of the Lord's name is known as 'blasphemy'. Though it is endemic in society, it is completely inappropriate behaviour for Christians. It abuses the name of the Lord as if he had no feelings. How would *we* feel if people started to use our names as swear words? – if, when they were angry, frustrated or showing off, they peppered their conversation with bitter cries of 'Norman!' or whatever? That's not how we would expect our friends to behave, and it's not how the Lord expects us to behave towards him.

Most of the phrases used to blaspheme in English started out as sincere expressions of the faithful. People called on the name of the Lord in times of danger. They implored others to act rightly 'for God's sake' (literally). But now, when the name of the Lord is invoked without any desire to involve his person, it simply serves to communicate that we care nothing for him or his feelings. It communicates that we couldn't really care less about *him*.

Blaspheming in this way cheapens the name of the Lord; it drags his name in the gutter. In a practical way it demonstrates faithlessness. It shows that the blasphemer regards the name of the Lord as just a word, and not as the name of a dearly loved and reverently feared friend.

Swearing isn't the only way of misusing the name of the Lord. It's possible, without a single swear word, to have a laugh at God's expense: to speak about the most precious things in the universe as if they were just the convenient butt of our jokes. We dishonour God when we turn him into a caricature, when we parody his Word, when we overdo the irony and laugh knowingly at the one without whom we would know nothing. That's not a fitting way for creatures to speak of their Creator, and it certainly isn't an appropriate way for Christians to carry on. 'Among you there must not be even a hint of ... foolish talk or coarse joking, which are out of place, but rather thanksgiving,' writes Paul (Ephesians 5:3–4).

Yet another way to dishonour the name of the Lord is to claim that he has told us something when he has not. 'God told me to do such and such,' we may say, when the reality is that we just feel like doing it. This kind of 'God told me' talk may sound holy and make us seem super-spiritual, but if it's not actually true we're seriously misusing God's name.

I've lost count of the number of times I've heard Christian believers claim that God has told them that something will happen, which then fails to happen. Some, to their credit, have immediately admitted that they were wrong in the first place. But others have responded by getting confused about why God seems to have changed his mind, or even by blaming God for failing to deliver on his promises. What a terrible charge to lay before our Father in heaven! We are weak, fallible sinners, who should always look to our own failings before we even think of pointing a finger at our Maker.

We go through life making mistakes. Sometimes they rebound on us and make us look foolish. But if we naïvely and carelessly put words in God's mouth, when things start to go wrong you can be sure that God's reputation will suffer. So we should take great care in expressing decisions or our sense of guidance. Perhaps we wouldn't dream of using the Lord's name as a swear word, but do we misuse his name by quoting him as saying things that are actually our own ideas, and thereby setting him up for contradiction? 'God told me …' does not mean the same as 'I think …'

A bit of swearing, having a laugh, exaggerating our sense of guidance: they're only words. Does anyone really care?

God cares; it's *his* reputation we endanger. He's the one who suffers reproach. And he it is who will call us to account for our careless talk which reveals our couldn't-care-less attitude, as Jesus himself warned: 'I tell you that people will have to give account on the day of judgment for every careless word they have spoken' (Matthew 12:36).

We may like to think that verbal sins don't really count, but two of the Ten Commandments (the Third and the Ninth) identify sins of speaking for which the guilty will be judged. For the unrepentant, the Last Day will confirm the old Second World War adage: 'Careless talk costs lives.'

Telling lives

It's not just what we say that communicates our attitude to God. How we live speaks volumes too. If we claim to be Christians but live like pagans, that sends a clear message to those around us. It conveys that we don't care about living to please God, or, even worse, that God doesn't care how we live. Since God is actually holy, and passionately opposed to sin, our careless behaviour communicates a lie about God. If we live shamelessly like this, we misuse the name of the Lord by calling ourselves Christians and bring dishonour on his name by our lives.

Six hundred people between the ages of eighteen and thirty were asked: 'What is the biggest obstacle that prevents you from believing in Christianity?' One of the respondents said: 'I became disillusioned with Christianity after many years of church attendance. I did not see many Christians (including the clergy) who actually followed the word of Christ.'[2] It is tragic that one of the biggest obstacles to faith in Christ is Christians.

It's easy to talk up a spiritual storm while living a completely worldly, selfish, Christless lifestyle. This kind of empty piety has been described as 'the loudest lie', and it is terrible that so many are influenced by its force. For St Augustine, 'to profess to love God while leading an unholy life is the worst of all falsehoods'. People judge God more by the sorry misrepresentation they see in our lives than by the pious words that come out of our mouths. Paul paraphrases Ezekiel 36:22: 'As it is written: "God's name is blasphemed among the Gentiles because of you"' (Romans 2:24). What a dreadful thought: that our lives might so distort the truth of who God is that his name comes to be blasphemed by those who see us!

Jesus reserved his sternest condemnation for people who talk like friends of God but live like his enemies. He called them 'hypocrites': 'Isaiah was right when he prophesied about you hypocrites; as it is written:

'"These people honour me with their lips,
  but their hearts are far from me."'
(Mark 7:6, quoting Isaiah 29:13)

It's not enough to talk Christian. We've got to *be* Christian. Remember our Lord's warning about the seriousness of all this: 'Not everyone who says to me, "Lord, Lord," will enter the kingdom of heaven, but only those who do the will of my Father who is in heaven' (Matthew 7:21).

It's easy to *sound* holy, but not so easy to *be* holy. That's why Paul calls us to examine ourselves to see whether we are in the faith (2 Corinthians 13:5). Hypocrisy comes so easily to us.

Peter was sure he was in the faith. He boasted to Jesus, 'Even if all fall away on account of you, I never will' (Matthew 26:33). But then Jesus was arrested and it became dangerous to be known as one of his followers. When Peter was recognized, he denied it with an oath: 'I don't know the man!' (Matthew 26:72).

The onlookers didn't believe him. They just saw someone who had been with Jesus, and who was now angrily swearing and trying to dissociate himself from the Lord. Peter's behaviour can hardly have increased the honour in which Jesus' name was held in Jerusalem!

It was an older, wiser Peter – a man personally confronted with his sin by Jesus, and forgiven – who wrote in his second letter:

> … make every effort to add to your faith goodness; and to goodness, knowledge; and to knowledge, self-control; and to self-control, perseverance; and to perseverance, godliness; and to godliness, mutual affection; and to mutual affection, love. For if you possess these qualities in increasing measure, they will keep you from being ineffective and unproductive in your knowledge of our Lord Jesus Christ. But if any of you do not have them, you are short-sighted and blind, and you have forgotten that you have been cleansed from your past sins (2 Peter 1:5–9).

Peter had learned the hard way that faithful words and faithful deeds are not the same, and that failure in either area can dishonour the name of the Lord. So now, in his second letter, he writes to warn believers against denying Jesus and to encourage them to tell the truth about him in their lives. We would do well to heed his words rather than repeating the great mistake of his life.

Misinformation technology
What has all this got to do with information technology? Nothing and everything.

It has nothing special to do with information technology because God's name can be dishonoured in any medium, just as his name can be (and should be) honoured in all media. But the Third Commandment has everything to do with information technology, because for the first time low-cost global publishing has been placed within reach of ordinary people. This means that our verbal sins can be relayed to an unprecedentedly large audience.

If I dishonour the name of the Lord while walking along the street with a friend, it will grieve the heart of the Lord, and that is a most awful thing. The only other person to hear and be affected by my utterance will be my friend. But if I email a friend with a new joke I've heard that pokes fun at God, my blasphemy could – if the joke is deemed funny enough by others – touch the lives of millions of people. The Lord's heart will be grieved that I have invoked his name without involving his person, but he will also be grieved that my folly has chipped away at the reverence of others for him.

Perhaps I think that the Lord has revealed something to me and, like Mary the mother of Jesus, I treasure up these things and ponder them privately in my heart (Luke 2:19). If I am right, the Lord will do what he has promised in his own time, and if I am wrong I will have learned an important lesson. But if I set up a website claiming that the Lord has revealed the future to me, and the events I foretell fail to materialize, what will happen? A substantial number of people will stumble on to my web page. Some of them will lay the blame at my door, writing me off as a religious maniac, a bit like members of those sects that go into the desert to await the end of the world at 3.27 next Tuesday afternoon. But for others, it will not be my reputation, but God's, that suffers. My mistake may confirm some in their scepticism and help to close the minds of others.

Whatever the medium, the message is the same: don't set God up for ridicule. The Bible tells us that some people will find the gospel of Jesus Christ ridiculous or offensive whatever we say or do (1 Corinthians 1:23; Matthew 13:57). But that does not give us licence to add insult to injury by broadcasting our own irreverence on the Internet. If people will mock the gospel, let them do so because they reject it, not because we have made a mockery of it for them. Let us take care how we behave in cyberspace, so that our contributions bring glory to God. Indeed, it may be appropriate actively to resist those who mock the Lord and dishonestly misrepresent him and his gospel, and to use the Web to set the facts straight.

The Third Net Commandment reminds us to watch our words in cyberspace, because the world is watching.

The Third Net Commandment

Do not say anything in cyberspace that misrepresents God or his gospel.

When Paul prayed for the young Christians in the Thessalonian church, he prayed that 'the name of our Lord Jesus may be glorified in you' (2 Thessalonians 1:12). We need to pray the same for ourselves and our churches in this age of mass communication.

Prayer

Lord, you hear every word I speak and write and type. You even know my secret thoughts. Please forgive me for the times my words have grieved you. Forgive me for the times I have dishonoured your name.

[Confess any specific instances that come to mind.]

Please help me to tell the truth about you in cyberspace and in real space. Guide me by your Spirit so that my words bring only honour to your name. And may the name of the Lord Jesus be glorified in me.

In his name I pray. Amen.

chapter 4

Sacred to God

Remember the Sabbath day by keeping it holy. Six days
you shall labour and do all your work, but the seventh
day is a Sabbath to the LORD your God. On it you shall
not do any work, neither you, nor your son or daughter,
nor your male or female servant, nor your animals, nor
the alien within your gates. For in six days the LORD
made the heavens and the earth, the sea, and all that is
in them, but he rested on the seventh day. Therefore the
LORD blessed the Sabbath day and made it holy.
(Exodus 20:8–11)

I should probably have worked harder, but now here I was, approaching the deadline for handing in my computer science graduate dissertation, with lots of work still to do. I collected the notes, books and manuals I needed, sat down at the computer terminal and started to work. It took a while to get stuck in; I suppose if it had been easy I wouldn't have put things off for so long. But once going I was soon caught up in the fascination of the problem at hand. Non-nerds may be sceptical, but there can be something deeply satisfying about concentrating on a computing problem, mastering its complexities and developing an elegant solution.

Eventually, I finished, sat back, rubbed my eyes and looked at my watch. What I saw made me nearly fall off my chair. I had been sitting there for seventeen hours without a break! I'd had no food or drink, no exercise, not even a visit to the toilet. As my interest rose in what I was doing, I had simply stepped into the Land That Time Forgot, and lost all contact with the normal passage of the hours. Somehow I had even disengaged from the physical needs of my own body.

Seventeen hours is my personal record. I have never experienced a longer continuous period of 'zoning out' in front of a computer. But I have often lost shorter periods in this way. The phenomenon is not confined to working on a computer; it can also be a feature of computer-game playing, interacting in chat rooms and surfing the Internet.

Years later, in the research and development department of an exciting young computer company, we worked hard and played hard. After hours, and sometimes during working hours, we would play networked computer games from the (then) latest generation of graphically vivid action adventures, such as *Wolfenstein* or *Doom*. It was amazing how quickly three or four hours could vanish in this pursuit.

Some Christians are opposed to computer games in principle. I don't share this view. Play is a perfectly normal and healthy part of human development, and I can see no reason, biblical or pragmatic, why computer play should be singled out for special attack. This is not to say that every computer game on the market is worth playing. In chapter 6 we shall explore why it may be wise to avoid *some* computer games.

However benign a game may be in its content, there remains the danger that players will play it obsessively, and to the exclusion of other activities essential to a balanced, healthy life. This is the danger with which my colleagues and I flirted when we played computer games in the office. We spent all day writing computer programs and all evening playing networked computer games, and then some of my colleagues went home and spent much of the night logged on to the Internet or playing solo computer games.

Consider the case of Robin, a twenty-nine-year-old public relations consultant, whose normally disciplined and productive life changed dramatically after she discovered Internet chat rooms.

> In the morning, Robin hits the snooze button on her alarm several times before dragging herself out of bed. There's no time for morning jogs, and those leisurely breakfasts are gone, replaced by the bagel she grabs as she runs out the door. She arrives at work exhausted, and those bursts of creativity that once flowed easily on the job when her mind was fresh and clear seldom come to her anymore ... When she staggers home, she knows that she should go to bed early to catch up on her rest, but by 8.30 pm she's back in cyberspace, where she quickly forgets those rational ideas about sleep.
>
> 'One time,' Robin recalls, 'I stayed online so long that I heard the birds singing and could see the sun rising out my window before I realised it was 6 am – time to get up.'[1]

Robin's story is familiar to many computer users. Though individual interests vary, the experience of being sucked into the technological time warp is widespread. Time disappears in extended screen sessions; sleep deprivation sets in; other areas of life suffer.

Stewardship of time

The Bible has important things to say about time and how it should be used. In its very first chapter we see the Creator giving the first humans a job to do; this was a prescription for how to spend their time. They were to act as stewards, looking after God's creation. They were to spend their days as the Creator's delegated under-managers, maintaining the paths and glades of the Garden of Eden and looking after its livestock (Genesis 1:26–30).

From this we learn that *God believes in work*. Just as God affirms the value of committed relationships in Genesis 2:18 ('It is not good for the man to be alone'), so he affirms the value of occupation. It is as if he says, 'It is not good for the man and woman to have nothing to do.' God himself is a worker who loves to create and sustain, so we shouldn't be surprised that he expects those who have been made in his image to be constructively occupied.

The Lord shows us that he expects us to *use* time, not to *waste* it (Ephesians 5:15–16). But this is not the whole story, because the Lord also expects us to take regular breaks from our work, just as he did from his work of creation.

> By the seventh day God had finished the work he had been doing; so on the seventh day he rested from all his work. And God blessed the seventh day and made it holy, because on it he rested from all the work of creating that he had done (Genesis 2:2–3).

It seems a bit odd to read of God resting. Was he tired out after all his exertions in creation? Surely not! It doesn't make sense to think of the all-powerful one needing to recharge his batteries.

The answer lies in the word 'rest'. When we hear this word, we tend to think of stretching out on a sofa and having a snooze or sitting down for a cup of coffee in the midst of a busy day. But an older meaning of the word 'rest' in English is simply to 'stop'. What you do when you stop is up to you: you can eat, sleep, shop or play volleyball. The important thing is that you stop what you were doing and do something else.

On the seventh day, God stopped what he had been doing (creating) and began to do something else (sustaining his creation). This wasn't just a single happening with no wider significance. The Fourth Commandment tells us that God intended his actions to be a pattern for the human race: work for six days, then rest for one. This day of rest has a special name: the Sabbath.

Remember the Sabbath day

What does it mean to observe the Sabbath? This question has challenged the faithful ever since Moses descended from Mount Sinai with the tablets of stone.

Some people have understood it to be a day on which all normal activity must cease. In the period between the Old and New Testaments, Jewish rabbis, anxious to avoid breaking God's law, tried to codify acceptable Sabbath practice into a system of rules and prohibitions. For example, Isaiah 58:13 says, 'keep your feet from breaking the Sabbath'. How far could one walk without breaking this rule? This led to the fixing of the 'Sabbath day's walk' (Acts 1:12), the maximum distance it was deemed reasonable to walk on the Sabbath (about three-quarters of a mile).

The trouble with human elaborations of God's law is that they can be treated as an end in themselves, distracting people from the more important reality. For example, Exodus 34:21 prohibits gathering in the harvest on the Sabbath; people should rest instead. When the Pharisees saw Jesus' hungry disciples plucking and nibbling at some ears of corn as they walked beside a field, they regarded it as a technical infringement of the Sabbath code (Mark 2:23–24). Jesus was scornful of their rigid interpretation of the law. 'The Sabbath was made for people,' he said, 'not people for the Sabbath. So the Son of Man is Lord even of the Sabbath' (Mark 2:27–28).

The purpose of the Sabbath is not to burden people with nit-picking regulations; it is there for our greater good. Any attempt to regulate it with rules that bind people in a straitjacket of 'do nots' misses the point of the Sabbath.

One Sabbath day, Jesus was in the synagogue and so was a man with a deformed hand. By this time, Jesus had established a reputation for performing miraculous works of compassion and healing. The Pharisees watched him to see what would happen, since the Old Testament rules for observing the Sabbath forbade work on that day, and surely healing constituted 'work'.

Rather than debating the point, Jesus shamed his critics by asking them a question: 'Which is lawful on the Sabbath: to do good or to do evil, to save life or to kill?' (Mark 3:4).

There can be only one answer: to keep the Sabbath holy to God must require us to prefer good over evil, to save life rather than to kill. To do nothing when we have it in our power to do good, so as to satisfy the requirements of a religious code, is a very strange way to show reverence for God.

How shall we put this into practice and find a healthy balance between finding the rest to which God calls us and doing good when it is in our power? Here are two practical suggestions.

First, plan to take a regular Sabbath break from your routine work. If an opportunity to do good comes up on your Sabbath, by all means act according to the example of Jesus, but do not go out looking for acts of charity to do on your Sabbath. There will always be more need in the world than we are personally able to address. Do not use this as an excuse to neglect taking a Sabbath. Jesus didn't. He cared passionately about the needs of the poor, and said, 'You will always have the poor among you' (John 12:8). Yet he regularly took time off by himself to pray, and was to be found each Sabbath worshipping in the synagogue. Jesus shows us by his example the importance he placed on the Sabbath. Without rest and regular, deliberate focusing on the Lord as our purpose and our provider, our physical, mental and spiritual resources will soon run dangerously low. So plan to take a regular Sabbath.

Secondly, many Christians apply some simple rules of thumb to decide what they will do on their Sabbath and what to leave for another day. These have the status of practical helps, not tyrannical rules. For example, does the intended activity focus on the Lord and his church? Does it bring us rest and refreshment? Or is it an act of 'necessity or mercy' to help others (including all God's creatures)? If the answer to all these questions is 'No', then perhaps it's best to put it off for another day and concentrate on more constructive Sabbath activities: worshipping God, sharing fellowship with his people, catching up on valuable rest and showing Christian compassion.

The Sabbath plays a minor role in the lives of some Christians who, in practice, regard it as if it were relevant to the Old

Testament period alone. They act as though the Sabbath had passed its 'use-by' date, like the Old Testament's kosher food laws (Leviticus 11; Acts 10:9–19). 'It is for freedom that Christ has set us free,' they say, quoting Galatians 5:1, and make no effort to carve out a Sabbath from their busy schedules.

I'm not convinced we may dispense with the Sabbath quite so easily. If it was really supposed to be a temporary measure, why is it presented to us as a creation ordinance: that is, something God has set in place for us from the very beginning in Genesis 1? That suggests there is something foundational for the created order about the Sabbath.

And why should a call to remember the Sabbath be included in the Ten Commandments, if it has a limited shelf life? We are rightly happy to consider the other nine Commandments as timelessly valid; can we really delete one commandment without compromising the rest?

I believe the weight of scriptural evidence points to the Sabbath principle's being as valid today as it ever was. Key elements of this 'Sabbath principle' are regular rest, worship and fellowship. The Sabbath should remind us of our absolute dependence on the Lord. He is our source of life and all things. The world will not stop turning if I take a little time off work, because it crucially depends on him, not on me. And if I stop meeting together in fellowship with other Christians, I can all too quickly forget that I am just one part of a larger family, the body of Christ, the church. Without the help, encouragement and example of my brothers and sisters I am at risk of developing a lopsided, idiosyncratic faith, or even of wandering from the path of faith altogether.

Rest, worship and fellowship are intrinsic to a healthy lifestyle, and are the God-given counterbalance to work.

Cyber-skiving

Before we turn to consider in more detail the temptations new technology puts in our path *not* to observe the Sabbath, let us pause to note the ways in which we can be tempted to use it to take *more* rest from work than is appropriate.

Someone recently sent me a postcard showing the following office timetable:

9.00	Starting time
9.30	Arrive at work
9.45	Coffee break
11.00	Check email
11.15	Prepare for lunch
12.00	Lunch
2.45	Browse the Internet
3.00	Tea break
4.00	Prepare to go home
4.30	Go home
5.00	Finishing time

Though this is a piece of tongue-in-cheek fun, it is not so far from how many people view their work. True, some jobs are inherently more interesting than others, and some privileged people actually get paid to do what they are passionate about and would gladly do for free. But most of us end up having at least some first-hand experience of the 'curse' of work, as expressed in God's words to Adam:

'Cursed is the ground because of you;
　　through painful toil you will eat of it
　　all the days of your life ...
By the sweat of your brow
　　you will eat your food ...'

(Genesis 3:17–19)

Some work is just plain hard: physically hard, mentally hard, emotionally hard. Some is mind-numbingly boring and repetit- ive. And some work can be extremely stressful. The introduction of the computer into the workplace has certainly eliminated some of the 'sweat' and 'painful toil' associated with old ways of doing things. For example, automation and robotics have killed off many unpleasant, or even dangerous, labour-intensive factory processes. But IT has not come without a price. A series of studies over recent years has demonstrated how new communications technologies are fuelling dangerous levels of workplace stress, with an alarming percentage of office workers succumbing to severe 'information overload' through email, fax, telephone, voice mail, SMS and Internet chat, not to mention good, old-fashioned snail mail. With every survey published, it seems that the percentage of workers having to process more than 100 messages per day increases. (That means each message must be processed and filed in under five minutes, if all the worker does all day is process messages.)

As if the stresses of information overload were not enough, it has also been found that some particular features of computing technology lead directly to heightened stress levels in users. According to a survey of 1,200 university and college students carried out by Dr Richard Hudiburg, an associate professor of psychology at the University of North Alabama, around 25% suffer some form of 'technostress' measured on a 'computer hassles' scale. Hudiburg compiled a list of thirty-seven factors causing stress in human-computer interaction. These include:

- Computer system is down
- Poorly documented software
- Hardware failure
- Keyboard paralysis
- Poor user interface
- Slow computer speed
- Incomprehensible error messages
- Crashed program
- Forgot to save work

Students experienced technostress in the form of irritability, anxiety, headaches, upset stomachs, nightmares, insomnia and fourteen other measurable physical or psychological complaints. 'The perceived lack of control itself can cause stress,' he concludes. 'There is a fear that change is going to take place and somehow we're going to be left behind. So we have less time on our hands because we're trying to do more. One of the things that was promised with computers was that we were going to have a lot more time on our hands and be able to relax and do other things, but the opposite is probably true.'[2]

Whether through stress or boredom, many workers (and students) are turning for light relief to the computer for recreational use during working hours. This can take a variety of forms, the most prevalent of which are:

- Sending private emails in work time
- Playing computer games (solo or on a network)
- Surfing the web
- Participating in online chat

So prevalent are these 'cyber-skiving' activities that they can have a serious impact on the productivity and profitability of businesses. In a survey carried out soon after the 'Web revolution' first impacted British businesses, cyber-skiving was the single biggest area of concern associated with the introduction of the Internet to the workplace.[3]

In a recent investigation into the work patterns of 16,000 staff at the US Internal Revenue Service, it was found that just over half the time they spent on the Internet had nothing whatever to do with work, and neither had half of their incoming emails. They spent 51% of their online time surfing for pornography, gambling or trading shares. The reason the survey was ordered in the first place was that one third of all telephone calls from the public received no answer. Customer service standards were being seriously impacted by the widespread cyber-skiving practices of staff.[4]

Just as it is inappropriate to work too much, so it is inappropriate to work too little, especially when someone else is paying. The attractions of cyber-skiving are obvious: the Internet can be a fascinating place and may be much more interesting than the workplace. It is also possible to explore it while sitting in front of the PC looking busy.

However tempting it may be, cyber-skiving is not an appropriate way for Christians to recharge their batteries. The Christian way is to take a proper Sabbath rest when work is done, but to work hard when it's time to work. Paul gives us some powerful motivation: 'Slaves, obey your earthly masters with respect and fear, and with sincerity of heart, just as you would obey Christ. Obey them not only to win their favour when their eye is on you, but like slaves of Christ, doing the will of God from your heart. Serve wholeheartedly, as if you were serving the Lord, not people' (Ephesians 6:5–7).

Online addiction

At the opposite end of the spectrum from cyber-skiving, many people are getting obsessively caught up in IT activities. The psychologist Dr Kimberley Young drew on the same criteria used to diagnose addictions such as compulsive gambling and alcoholism to devise a short questionnaire which she invited subjects in Internet discussion forums to complete. The questions included these:

- Do you feel preoccupied with the Internet (i.e. think about previous online activity or anticipate the next online session)?
- Do you feel the need to use the Internet with increasing amounts of time in order to achieve satisfaction?
- Have you repeatedly made unsuccessful efforts to control, cut back or stop Internet use?
- Do you feel restless, moody, depressed, or irritable when attempting to cut down or stop Internet use?
- Do you stay online longer than originally intended?
- Have you jeopardized or risked the loss of a significant relationship, job, educational or career opportunity because of the Internet?
- Have you lied to family members, a therapist or

others to conceal the extent of your involvement
with the Internet?
- Do you use the Internet as a way of escaping
from problems or of relieving a distressed mood
(e.g. feelings of helplessness, guilt, anxiety,
depression)?

Out of the 496 respondents, Dr Young categorized 396 (80%) as Internet addicts![5] Some commentators question the possibility of a person's becoming addicted to a *machine*, and suggest that talk of 'addiction' is alarmist. Dr Young and a growing number of researchers beg to differ, claiming extensive evidence of the same kinds of psychological dependence in Internet addicts as is normally found in people with chemical and social addictions. Hospital clinics to treat computer and Internet addiction are now starting to appear in the USA.

First-hand testimonies of the families and loved ones of Internet addicts certainly read like instances of classical addiction. Here is a letter sent to Dr Young by the spouse of an Internet addict (drawn from a substantial archive of similar material):

My wife spends more than 40 hours a week playing these fantasy role-playing games on the Internet. Her 'virtual life' has left our marriage and family in shambles. All she wants to do is play the game. A man she met on-line got her address and is sending her very strange and personal letters. I'm afraid she may leave. Our pastor does not know how to help. Can you suggest anything I can do to bring her back to reality? Our whole family is really hurting ...[6]

As in better-known addictions, loved ones have a sense of 'losing' the addict to their craving and its subculture. Their time and attention get siphoned away from normal life, leaving the addict exhausted and loved ones distraught. Here is a Top Ten list of activities most commonly reported to suffer because of Internet addiction:

1. Time with partner or family
2. Daily chores
3. Sleep
4. Reading
5. Watching TV
6. Time with friends
7. Exercise
8. Hobbies
9. Sex
10. Social events[7]

Where in all this is the addict's spiritual life? With better-known addictions, the impact on spiritual health can be devastating. The First Commandment requires God to be first in our lives, but the addict's urges cry out for the object of addiction to have that position.

There are no easy answers for addicts or their loved ones. Honesty is vital; if you don't admit there's a problem you can't do anything about it. Seek the help of wise Christians, medical professionals and trusted friends. Most of all, seek the Lord's help in prayer. Jesus came to 'proclaim freedom for the prisoners' and to 'release the oppressed' (Luke 4:18). 'Come to me, all you who are weary and burdened,' he said, 'and I will give you rest' (Matthew 11:28).

We all need the Lord's rest in our lives, whether we are full-blown Internet addicts or just heavy users of the technology. A vital question for us is this: 'Is my use of this technology interfering with the peace I have in Christ Jesus?' If so, it doesn't necessarily signal a need to renounce the technology, but it ought to prompt us to take stock and examine our lives to see where they have got out of balance. A lifestyle that is healthy for mind, body and spirit will include a range of activities, with God taking first place in all of them, and no activity monopolizing an unreasonable amount of time.

A time for everything

Scripture presents a beautiful picture of the different components of a healthy life, each appropriate for its proper season, but
none appropriate as the only activity in life:

> There is a time for everything,
>> and a season for every activity under heaven:
>
>> a time to be born and a time to die,
>> a time to plant and a time to uproot,
>> a time to kill and a time to heal,
>> a time to tear down and a time to build,
>> a time to weep and a time to laugh,
>> a time to mourn and a time to dance,
>> a time to scatter stones and a time to gather them,
>> a time to embrace and a time to refrain,
>> a time to search and a time to give up,
>> a time to keep and a time to throw away,
>> a time to tear and a time to mend,
>> a time to be silent and a time to speak,
>> a time to love and a time to hate,
>> a time for war and a time for peace.
>
> (Ecclesiastes 3:1–8)

In the spirit of the Fourth Commandment, the Fourth Net
Commandment is concerned with getting the balance right
between computer use and other activities, while being absolutely clear about the need to ring-fence priority time for nurtur-
ing our relationship with our heavenly Father:

The Fourth Net Commandment

Do not get into addictive patterns of computer use: set
aside regular off-line time that is sacred to God and
non-negotiable.

Prayer

Lord, thank you for all the good things about new technology. Help me to enjoy them, and to remember to thank you for them. Please help me to be wise in my use of time, in the discipline of my thought life, and in the balance of activities I pursue. Help me to be able to set other things aside regularly to spend quality time with you.

[Bring to the Lord any special problems you've struggled with, asking for his help.]

Please enable me to accomplish the good works you've prepared in advance for me to do, and help me not to waste the precious time you've given me. Thank you, Lord.

In Jesus' name. Amen.

chapter 5

The generation gap

*Honour your father and your mother, so that you may
live long in the land the LORD your God is giving you.*
(Exodus 20:12)

Here's how the world works: the old teach the young. Those who
have passed their exams at the School of Hard Knocks and gradu-
ated from the University of Life simply have deeper reserves of
experience to draw on. They have had longer to reflect on the
lessons of their own lives and those of previous generations, and are
thus less likely to make silly mistakes. A young person who wants to
be wise should listen to the accumulated wisdom of the older generation, who hold the lessons of the past in trust for the younger.

The writer of the early part of the biblical book of Proverbs
certainly seems to see things this way:

> Listen, my sons, to a father's instruction;
>> pay attention and gain understanding.
> I give you sound learning,
>> so do not forsake my teaching.
> When I was a boy in my father's house,
>> still tender, and an only child of my mother,

he taught me and said,
'Lay hold of my words with all your heart;
keep my commands and you will live.'

(Proverbs 4:1–4)

This isn't just recounted as a personal testimony; it's offered as a principle to be applied:

Train children in the way they should go,
and when they are old they will not turn from it.

(Proverbs 22:6)

Neither is the principle intended to be restricted to relationships between adults and children. Paul encourages Titus to support the older women in the church, so that by their lives and their words they can 'train the younger women' (Titus 2:3–4).

The old teach the young; it's how the world works.

The generation gap

At least, that's how the older generation sees things; the younger generation has never been entirely convinced. After all, young people reason, how seriously can we take the generation that bequeathed us war, injustice, poverty, environmental degradation and Third World debt? No, the future belongs to the young, and it is the young – not the old – who are our best hope.

And so the generation gap opens up. The old think the young are ignorant (because they have experienced so little) and foolish (because they don't realize it). The young think the old are guilty (because they have not done enough, or have done the wrong things) and foolish (because they don't realize it).

The weapons employed in the revolution of young against old are many and varied: hairstyles or fashions chosen to be as far removed from parental preferences as possible, life choices defined more by what they react against than by their intrinsic worth, and, of course, screaming rows.

Queen Victoria, who had many children and grandchildren, once observed, 'You will find as the children grow up that as a rule children are a bitter disappointment – their greatest object being to do precisely what their parents do not wish and have anxiously tried to prevent.'[1] For their part, children struggle, not just with the greater power society invests in their elders, but also with the perceived inadequacies of their parents. This is exacerbated by the knowledge that we ourselves are profoundly shaped by our parents, both in our genes and in our behaviour. Our generation-gap anger is fuelled by the fear that we may be personally blighted by our parents' failings.

Freudian psychology takes the complex love/hate relationships between parents and young children as one of the primary formative influences on personality and emotional outlook. So if we feel emotionally damaged, why not blame our parents? This is a common conscious or subconscious chain of reasoning. In the words of Oscar Wilde, 'Children begin by loving their parents; after a time they judge them; rarely, if ever, do they forgive them.'[2]

The Bible has much to say about the generation gap, and it doesn't shrink from showing us examples of outright generation war. One of the most extreme cases is the rebellion by King David's son Absalom against his father (2 Samuel 13 – 18). While the rest of the people of Israel regarded David as a hero, his own son thought he was a fool who deserved to be replaced as king by someone who *really* knew what he was doing: you've guessed it – Absalom himself! David's paternal love for his son blinded him to the sheer, calculating venom of the younger man, until the king had to flee for his life from his own son. Eventually, the rebellion cost Absalom his life, and King David – who only just held on to his throne – was heartbroken. There are no winners in the generation war.

Jesus himself endorsed the command to honour parents (see Matthew 15:3–6; Mark 7:9–13), and he honoured his own Father (John 8:49). In Luke 15:11–32 he told a famous generation-gap story. The prodigal son outrageously demanded his share of his father's inheritance before the old man had even died! Amazingly, he got it, and promptly left to do everything his father had warned him not to do. He stayed out late, went clubbing and hung out with loose women. He probably even grew his hair the way that would annoy his father most.

Once again, one of the lessons of the story is that generation war always ends in tears. The young man's money ran out and his fair-weather friends fell away. But, unlike the story of Absalom, this story moves on to the forgiveness and restoration that can follow when there is repentance and love to heal the generational breakdown.

> The son said to him, 'Father, I have sinned against heaven and against you. I am no longer worthy to be called your son.'
>   But the father said to his servants, 'Quick! Bring the best robe and put it on him. Put a ring on his finger and sandals on his feet. Bring the fattened calf and kill it. Let's have a feast and celebrate. For this son of mine was dead and is alive again; he was lost and is found' (Luke 15:21–24).

It's clear that Jesus intended the story of the prodigal son to be understood as a picture of the grace of God, our heavenly Father, towards rebels like us if we repent. Perhaps the story of Absalom, while an account of an actual historical event, is included in the Bible partly to give us a picture of how a human father loves and grieves over a rebel child, and thus to remind us of how profoundly our heavenly Father loves and grieves over us when we rebel.

This may also be why this, the first of the Ten Commandments not to refer directly to how we relate to God, calls us to honour our parents. The First Commandment requires that God must be first in our lives, the Second that he should not have any rivals, the Third that we should honour his name, and the Fourth that we should rest in reliance on him. But the Fifth Commandment sets out a rule for how people should relate to other people. If we do not learn to respect the greater life experience of our parents and, more importantly, the sacrificial love they have shown us over many years, how shall we ever learn to love our

Father in heaven? Yes, it *is* easier to honour model parents than deeply flawed parents who have neglected, abused or abandoned us, but this commandment does not say, 'Honour your father and your mother if they've been pretty near perfect.'

We should be slow to judge or condemn our parents, or anyone in the older generation. Rather, the Bible encourages us to 'show respect for the elderly' (Leviticus 19:32). They have travelled the same road as we have, and may remember what it was like to feel frustration with *their* older generation. But they have arrived at a higher vantage point, and their longer view leads them to see things differently. We may think that that could never happen to us, but the conflict between generations is 'the one war in which everyone changes sides'.[3] As the apostle Paul reflected: 'When I was a child, I talked like a child, I thought like a child, I reasoned like a child. When I became an adult, I put childish ways behind me' (1 Corinthians 13:11).

No doubt similar observations could be made by people looking back on every transition from one stage of life to the next. The 'middle-aged perspective' seems foolish only until the observer reaches middle age, when it begins to seem like the only sensible way to see things. Mark Twain recognized the experience in his own life: 'When I was a boy of 14, my father was so ignorant I could hardly stand to have the old man around. But when I got to be 21, I was astonished at how much the old man had learned in seven years.'[4]

Older people may feel threatened by the energy and openness to change of the younger generation, but perhaps the single most significant reality underlying the generation gap is that older people genuinely know more than younger people – a fact that younger people often resent or seek to deny.

What would happen if this longstanding inbuilt advantage for the older generation were to be swept away?

The generation lap
Many people believe that this extraordinary reversal has already taken place in the arena of new technology. Don Tapscott has written best-selling books chronicling the changes taking place in

society as it engages with new information technologies. In his book *Growing Up Digital: The Rise of the Net Generation*, he examines the lives and outlooks of young people who have never known what life without the Internet is like.

> When it comes to understanding and using the new media and technology, many parents are falling woefully behind their children. We've shifted from a generation gap to a *generation lap* – kids outpacing and overtaking adults on the technology track, *lapping* them in many areas of daily life ... Society has never before experienced this phenomenon of the knowledge hierarchy being so effectively flipped on its head. But it is definitely happening and the situation is magnified with each new technology.[5]

While parents struggle with the basic concepts of new technology, members of the Net Generation don't even notice that it's there. It has been said that technology is 'technology only for people who are born before it was invented'.[6] 'That's why we don't argue about whether the piano is corrupting music with technology.'[7]

Even the simplest matters for younger users can prove challenging for their elders. The former US Secretary of State, Madeleine Albright, was invited to participate in an online chat session at the American Library in Moscow. She struggled while school students from forty-eight countries waited to talk to her online, confessing, 'I do know how to type, but I am not good at the mouse. People of a certain age do not have very good eye–hand co-ordination.'[8]

'Tech stuff is natural for me, it takes me a minute to set up a computer. It takes my parents an hour.' So says an unnamed fourteen-year-old boy in Tapscott's *Growing Up Digital.*[9] The Internet is full of tales relating the prize idiocies of those for whom computers are 'a riddle wrapped in a mystery inside an enigma'.[10] They work as humour to those in the know by drawing attention to the ignorance of those who haven't a clue.

Parents do not typically mock the ignorance of their children; what else would we expect from those who are still so young? But it seems harder to accept the ignorance of an older generation. A common reaction is that our parents really ought to know better. 'My mother can't even enter Windows without step-by-step instructions,' says twelve-year-old Dectrice with disdain.[11]

Writing in the 1930s, the renowned psychologist Carl Jung sided with the younger generation when he said: 'Our whole educational problem suffers from a one-sided approach to the child who is to be educated, and from an equally one-sided lack of emphasis on the uneducatedness of the educator.'[12]

John Seely Brown, Chief Scientist at Xerox's Palo Alto Research Center, offers this analysis: 'This is a unique period in history in that the role of the child in the home is changing ... For the first time there are things that parents want to be able to know about and do, where the kids are, in fact, the authority.'[13]

This reversal is dramatically illustrated by a government initiative in Finland, where 5,000 school pupils were selected to train the country's teachers in how to use computers. 'For the first time ever, in one domain, the students will be the teachers and the teachers will be the students. The power dynamic between students and teachers will be forever altered.'[14]

This shift in knowledge and power can be seen to have both positive and negative effects. It has always been the case that those who are older can learn from those who are younger. Jesus used the characteristic trust and dependence of little children as an object lesson for people of all ages (Matthew 18:3). The realization by young people that they possess expertise that older people value and need can bring a healthy sense of dignity. As sixteen-year-old Kim Devereaux says: 'I think that technology has changed the way adults treat me. They seem to take my opinions more seriously because they realise I just may know something they don't.'[15]

Conversely, there is a temptation for younger people – who have always been tempted to think they know better than their elders – to take the fact that they really *do* know better in the area of technology as a licence to treat their elders with contempt, ridiculing their ignorance and keeping them ignorant by over-mystifying explanations. For the cynical young fighter in the generation war, the technology divide furnishes ample ammunition to fuel hostilities.

On the other side of the barricades, the awareness that young people inhabit a different and unfamiliar mental space can be a source of great concern. Not knowing what it is you don't know means you have no idea whether it's dangerous or not. The opinion research company Roper Starch has documented a dramatic increase in concern among US adults about young people. In 1991, 11% said that their biggest concern was 'the way young people think and act'. This grew to 23% in 1993 and 34% in 1997. This means that the chief concern in life of more than one third of US adults is that they can't relate to young people's thinking and consequent action. It is difficult to identify the causes of the dramatic upturn in this area of concern during the 1990s, but surely the rise of new technology must play a significant role.

No-one likes to be seen to be stupid, and, for many people, being shown up by the superior skill or knowledge of a younger person ranks as a truly terrible humiliation. Perhaps this is why some adults resist the obvious fact that younger people are more accomplished computer users than they, and sometimes they may even blame them for their abilities. Mike Uttech, aged thirteen, describes the mixed reactions his computer skills evoke:

> I have some teachers who won't accept the fact that a student knows more about something than they do. Some of my teachers love me to help out with tasks – whether it is saving files to disks, printing or other tasks. But other teachers think I'm being rude knowing more than they do. I also find it funny when a teacher won't let me help and then gets the computer specialist at the school to do it. I think that the teachers and adults should listen to us more and maybe even learn something from us.[16]

Surely Mike is right. Knowledge of computers is not like the wisdom that only decades of life can bring. Younger people have a massive advantage over their elders. Apart from pride, there is no reason why an older person should not gladly learn lessons in technology from a younger instructor, and, properly handled, such sessions have the potential to be rich times of growing trust and relationship across the generations.

Bridging the generation gap

People differ in ages, in life experience and in many other ways, so some kind of generation gap is inevitable. But there is nothing inevitable about the generation war. Christian love is not sectarian; it does not say, 'I will love only people just like me.' Christian love is extravagant, reaching out with equal passion to those who differ from us in race, creed, colour, nationality, gender and, yes, age. The church is not a social club for those who would naturally choose to be together; it is a richly textured family of disparate individuals united in Christ Jesus. Diversity is not something to be feared in the church, but rather celebrated (e.g. 1 Corinthians 12:12–31). So it is wholly inappropriate for older people to find excuses to belittle the young, or for younger people to write off their out-of-touch elders.

For Christians, relationships between the generations should be characterized by respect, patience, understanding and appreciation of the distinctive strengths of people at different stages of life. If this is true in the Christian family at large, how much more important that these traits should be found within specific families! This is how Paul expresses the balance: 'Children, obey your parents in everything, for this pleases the Lord. Parents, do not embitter your children, or they will become discouraged' (Colossians 3:20–21).

The Bible envisages a healthy and loving interdependence between the generations throughout life:

- Parents give the gift of life to their children through conception and birth.

- Parents nurture, care for and educate children through childhood and adolescence.
- Wise children recognize their parents' sacrifice and honour them by trusting them and recognizing their greater authority.
- Parents and children share adult companionship for a time.
- Children end up returning the care and love shown to them by looking after their parents as they get older.

Many people's actual experience of family life falls short of this ideal, but the challenge to all Christians is to find ways of doing our part to bring the love of Christ into relationships across the generations. We cannot change the history of our families, and we cannot make other people's decisions for them, but we can take a principled decision to show respect rather than contempt, and to leave judging where it belongs: with God alone.

The Fifth Commandment has a very practical application in relation to new technology. We can express it in these terms:

The Fifth Net Commandment

Do not use your knowledge of new technology to humiliate the older generation.

Prayer

Heavenly Father, thank you for making me your child. Thank you for revealing things to me that I could never have discovered by myself. I'm sorry for the times I've rebelled against your authority, and failed to honour you. Please forgive me for those failures, and also for the occasions when I've rejected the good example or advice of people you've given me to build me up. Forgive me for when I've treated older people or parents badly for my own selfish reasons.

[Confess any specific instances that come to mind.]

Please help me to be humble and generous in my relationships (especially with my parents). Help me not to use what I know about new technology or anything else as a weapon to hurt people, but rather as a tool to serve you and to help them.

In Jesus' name. Amen.

chapter 6

Death to hacking

You shall not murder.
(Exodus 20:13)

If any early-morning commuters on their way to work in
Cambridge, Massachusetts, on the morning of 9 May 1994
chanced to look up, they would have seen a most unusual sight.
Parked high on top of the 'Great Dome' of the Massachusetts
Institute of Technology (MIT) was what appeared to be a real
police car, complete with flashing lights. Inside the car was a life-
like dummy wearing a police uniform. On the windscreen was an
MIT Campus Police parking ticket ('No permit for this location'). It would be impossible for a car to be driven up on to the
domed roof, and the heavy machinery necessary to lift it would
have attracted attention from the authorities. But, somehow, the
car had been smuggled up there during the night, without
anyone noticing.

What was undoubtedly a puzzle for passers-by would immediately have been understood by MIT students and staff as the
latest example of a long-running series of high-profile, technically ingenious and resolutely benign practical jokes known in
MIT parlance as 'hacks'.[1] Over many years, a set of guiding

principles has evolved to ensure that hacks retain their gently
amusing character, without descending into malicious or dangerous territory. Anything failing to comply with the 'Hacker
Ethic' would probably not be considered a 'hack' in the MIT
community.

> *The Hacker Ethic*
> A hack must
> - be safe
> - not damage anything
> - not damage anyone, physically, mentally or
>   emotionally
> - be funny, at least to most of the people who
>   experience it[2]

MIT has played a formative role in the development of the
electronic computer from its earliest days, and continues to be at
the leading edge of technological innovation. It should not come
as any surprise, then, that the people at MIT who displayed bril-
liantly creative, somewhat unorthodox technical abilities to coax
unexpected results from the first lumbering computers came to
be known as 'hackers'. Sherry Turkle, a sociology professor at
MIT, has documented some of the social changes that contact
with new technologies has brought about, using the academic
community on her own doorstep as a source of data:

> The hacker subculture was made up of programmer-
> virtuosos who were interested in taking large, complex
> computer systems and pushing them to their limits.
> Hackers could revel in the imperfectly understood. As
> they programmed, things did not always get clearer,
> but they became workable, at least for the master
> hacker with the 'right stuff'. Hacking offered a certain
> thrill-seeking, a certain danger. It provided the sense,
> as one hacker put it, 'of walking on the edge of a cliff'.
> He explained further, 'You could never really know
> that your next little "local fix" wouldn't send the whole

system crashing down on you.' The hacker style made an art form of navigating the complexity of opaque computer microworlds.[3]

However precarious and potentially destructive this kind of engineering may have been, its motivation was constructive. The objective was to tame the system, to harness its power and put it to work, not to break it or cause inconvenience to others. The pioneering hackers in the MIT computer lab followed a tacit code every bit as positive in outlook as the MIT Hacker Ethic.

Over the years there has been a certain amount of blurring of the boundaries between the two senses of 'hacking' at MIT. On April Fool's Day, 1998, hackers broke into the MIT Web server and changed the official MIT home page to include the headline 'Walt Disney Corporation to Acquire MIT for $6.9 Billion' over a picture of Mickey Mouse pointing to the Great Dome with Mickey Mouse ears on it. The college authorities – though somewhat embarrassed – clearly considered that this hack complied with the Hacker Ethic (i.e. they found it funny). They allowed the spoof page to remain on the official website for the rest of the day and promptly issued an official press release observing that it had been obvious that the story was a prank, as $6.9 billion was much too low a price to pay for the institution!

In the rarefied environment of MIT, 'hacking' continues to be understood as a clever, creative, technically sophisticated, and sometimes downright funny activity. But throughout the rest of the world the term has come to signify a much darker application of technical skill, in which hackers seek their thrills not by spreading mirth but by spreading terror; not by solving problems but by causing them.[4]

It isn't funny any more

The 1983 film *War Games*, starring a very youthful Matthew Broderick, tells the story of a teenage hacker who likes to break into other people's computer systems just for kicks. Technotrespass is a common source of adrenalin buzz for hackers. Just as there are some people who can't see a high wall without wanting to know what's on the other side, so there are many who can't see a network firewall[5] without experiencing the same sense of curiosity. The hacker who recently broke into the private files of Microsoft Chairman Bill Gates and ordered him a consignment of Viagra, using Gates's own credit card, was just one, highly publicized, example of what thousands of people try to do every day.

A whole hacker sub-culture has sprung up with its own conventions and jargon. 'Script kiddies' are people – typically males in their teens or early twenties – who use programme scripts to scan the Internet looking for computers with known vulnerabilities. Anyone with a personal firewall running on their computer will know just how often someone out there tries to break into even the humble home computer. The real targets, though, are not ordinary individuals, but large organizations. A friend of mine was responsible for managing the network security of a multinational organization whose network sustains on average more than 30,000 attacks per day!

A variety of motives drives hackers to try to breach network security. A desire for personal gain is certainly one motivation. We shall look at this in more detail in chapter 8. Others want to penetrate the systems of target organizations so as to wreak destruction, whether for reasons of political ideology, personal revenge or a simple lust for vandalism. The majority want to break in out of straightforward nosiness (they want to see what's there), or because they see it as a challenge (because it's there).

The young hacker in *War Games* is simply exploring what's out there when he stumbles on a vast online war game. Naturally, he joins in the game, and plays enthusiastically until the awful moment when he realizes that it's not a game, but rather the US military's central battlefield command system, and he has just brought the world to the brink of the Third World War. The film highlights the folly of automating difficult decisions that call for human understanding and the exercise of moral judgment. It also shows how disastrously wrong a little 'innocent' hacking could go.

Critics will protest that *War Games* used fictional licence to exaggerate the dangers, but a substantial body of evidence accumulated over the years since the film was made tend to render it more, not less, plausible. In 1997 a British court fined a nineteen-year-old student £1,000 for downloading dozens of top-secret files from the US Griffiths Air Force Base and from Lockheed, the missile and aircraft manufacturer. The scale of the punishment indicates the court's belief that this was an act of mischief, not espionage, but the fact remains that the student was snooping around inside a supposedly secure network including the management of lethal weaponry.

The space agency NASA experiences more than 500,000 cyber attacks per year. There is evidence that a hacker attack compromised the safety of Space Shuttle astronauts in an incident in 1997. Robert Gross, Inspector General at NASA, is reported to have said, 'We had an activity at a NASA centre where a hacker was overloading our systems ... to such an extent that it interfered with communications between the NASA Centre, some medical communications and the astronaut aboard the Shuttle.' When asked how dangerous this kind of attack was, Gross replied, 'It shows the potential that hackers have for doing some real damage to NASA's mission and astronaut safety.'[6]

In a world where so much of our medical, transport, energy, communications and defence infrastructure is controlled by networked computers, even a well-meaning hacker driven by no more than curiosity has the potential to do serious, even fatal, damage.

Virus wars

At its simplest, a computer virus is a program that clones itself at every opportunity, with every clone behaving in the same way. It passes from computer to computer via disks, email or other links, and, thanks to the massive interconnectedness of today's computer systems, it can spread round the world many times faster than any human virus.

Some viruses target the computer systems they infect, jumbling up the stored memory data or even wiping the hard disk. On 15 November 1995, Christopher Pile, an unemployed twenty-six-year-old calling himself the 'Black Baron', became the first person to receive a prison sentence for writing and distributing a computer virus. Pile was responsible for the Pathogen and Queeg viruses, both of which wreaked considerable havoc. They were 'polymorphic', which means they changed some of their characteristics each time they reproduced, thereby making it hard for virus-checking software to detect them. Their effect was to erase all the data from the computers they infected, shortly after disabling the keyboard, so the horrified user could only watch helplessly as the taunting message appeared on their screens: 'Smoke me a kipper, I'll be back for breakfast ... unfortunately some of your data won't.'

Destructive viruses like Pile's are relatively uncommon. The majority are harmless to the computers they infect, leaving only a small trace of their visit, like an electronic 'Kilroy was here'. Their menace is that they clog up the Internet with junk mail to such an extent that all communications grind to a halt. For example, some viruses transmitted by email simply read the contents of the recipient's email address book and forward the virus to every address listed in it. (Notable examples include the Melissa and ILOVEYOU viruses.) If the average user has fifty addresses listed in his or her address book, it takes only four 'generations' of the virus to generate more than six million email messages (6.25 million, to be precise). In ten generations the virus will generate almost a million million million emails, none of them with any constructive purpose, but, taken together, enough to cripple the Internet and obstruct vital communications for days. It has been claimed that the cost to business when the ILOVEYOU virus crippled the Internet was $10 billion.

'Denial-of-service' attacks use a similar principle to crash web sites deliberately. The hacker writes a program to generate so many requests to the target website that the server running it crashes. Though many denial-of-service attacks are motivated by the usual hackers' quest to 'see if I can', I have personally witnessed a concerted denial-of-service attack from multiple originating sources working in concert in an attempt to vandalize a high-profile commercial website. It is difficult to prosecute cases of this kind through the courts, especially when the hackers operate across international boundaries, but all the evidence pointed to the attack being the work of a commercial competitor, trying to discredit the market leader.

Hacking for technophobes

It isn't even necessary to be a techno-whizz in order to start a virus. Email chain letters have a similar effect. They arrive unsolicited, they have minimal useful content, and they encourage users to pass the message on to everyone they know. The gullible user ends up doing the job of the virus program, and no virus protection software on earth can guard against such 'intentional' viruses.

I have noticed over the years that Christians seem to be particularly susceptible to certain kinds of low-tech virus. The first kind is the 'virus warning'. You receive an email from a trusted friend, who got it from someone they know. It purports to be a warning to be on the alert for a computer virus doing the rounds. Often the message includes a phrase such as 'A Microsoft spokesman this morning confirmed that …' (if not Microsoft, substitute IBM, Apple, HP, Dell, or whoever). Since the quote is never dated, it is impossible to know whether it really was *this* morning, or if the email has actually been doing the rounds for the last six months. The alleged virus is always said to be hidden in an email with the name *XYZ*, where *XYZ* is some apparently benign phrase. Here's the news: the warning *is* the virus. Pass it on and you spread the virus. Do nothing and you kill the virus.

Christians seem particularly susceptible to this kind of hoax, presumably because of a higher than average commitment to helping others. But Christians are also supposed to have a higher than average commitment to the truth, so, before passing on junk mail to everyone you know, it is wise to check whether the claim is really true. Reputable IT security websites such as www.mcafee.com and www.symantec.com keep an up-to-date list. I have a personal policy of never passing on virus alerts. These days, if the threat is real and widespread, the broadcast and print media will quickly publicize it.

Another form of low-tech, high-volume Net abuse goes by the

bizarre name of 'spamming'[7]. In normal life there are practical limits to the volumes of junk mail that get sent, imposed by the costs of paper, printing and postage. In cyberspace, the cost of sending a million messages is the same to the sender as the cost of sending one message. This makes it very tempting to inundate everyone in the world with messages promoting your own particular enthusiasm.

The acknowledged pioneers of over-the-top spam are Laurence Canter and Martha Siegel, a married team of Arizona lawyers. They sent unsolicited messages to more than 6,000 Usenet groups, offering to help immigrants enter a forthcoming 'Green Card lottery'. Usenet is a part of the Internet providing online discussion forums on thousands of topics. Each discussion is highly focused, and users tend to be fiercely protective of the need to keep the discussion to the main point. Whatever your hobby, enthusiasm, aversion or perversion, there is likely to be a Usenet group dedicated to that topic. Anyone introducing off-topic contributions is likely, at best, to receive polite requests to stick to the subject or, more likely, to be flamed. ('Flaming' is where Internet users send strongly worded – sometimes abusive – messages to users who, innocently or otherwise, violate the *de facto* code of practice of the users of that section of the Internet community.)

Canter and Siegel did nothing illegal, but they flagrantly violated the Usenet code when they intruded into discussions with their off-topic solicitations. 'The international outrage over Canter and Siegel's intrusion – regarded as doubly obnoxious because it was not done in the interests of sharing information but merely to make money – was immediate and overwhelming. So many angry protests were electronically dispatched to Canter and Siegel's Internet Service Provider that its host computers crashed more than fifteen times.'[8]

Far from being chastened by the experience, Canter and Siegel went on to launch further spams, became minor television celebrities and wrote a book entitled *How to Make a Fortune on the Information Superhighway*![9] But what they grasped with both hands as an opportunity was an irritation to millions, and caused serious inconvenience, and perhaps worse, to many people by crashing part of the Internet.

Hacking: the new sin?

In the Introduction we noted the remark in Douglas Coupland's novel *Microserfs*, that hackers 'invented a new sin'.[10] Hacking is certainly a new phenomenon, but is it truly a new sin? I don't believe so. It is only a new way to trespass on someone else's property, at best violating their privacy, at worst causing actual damage, whether by accident or design.

But perhaps there is more to it than disregard for property. In the world of flesh and blood, the most precious gift we have is our life. It is a truly terrible thing to murder a person, to take a life and wipe someone off the face of the earth. In cyberspace, our most precious commodity is information. The most hateful, harmful thing you can do to a person in cyberspace is to erase their information – to wipe their existence off the face of cyber-space. True, it's not ultimately as drastic as murdering the person in the flesh, but perhaps the impetus of the heart to wound, to destroy, to annul is not so far removed.

Some may protest that only a small minority of hackers act out of hatred; the majority are much more like MIT enthusiasts than urban terrorists. This may be true. Sociological studies of the cre-ators of viruses have found that most are highly educated, middle-to upper-middle-class, with a respect for authority, a contempt for hypocrisy, and healthy relationships with parents, friends and loved ones. What they do tends to be done for personal reasons rather than out of venom towards others. Christopher Pile (the 'Black Baron') said he wanted to raise his self-esteem by creating a British virus to rival foreign ones. The Bulgarian virus-writing legend known as the Dark Avenger gives an alternative explana-tion: 'I think the idea of making a program that would travel on its own, and go places its creator could never go, was the most interesting thing for me. The American government can stop me from going to the United States, but they can't stop my viruses.'[11]

It is worth noting how the distinction between murder and manslaughter is recognized in Old Testament law. Murder was absolutely prohibited, as the Sixth Commandment makes clear, and the penalty for guilt was death.

> Whoever sheds human blood, by human beings shall their blood be shed; for in the image of God has God created all people (Genesis 9:6).

But what if one person kills another accidentally? Should that person still be sentenced to death? The Old Testament has a way of affirming that the blood of the innocent victim cries out for retribution, while leaving room for the unintentional killer to escape with his or her life.

The law required the dead person's close relative to be appointed the 'avenger of blood'; his responsibility was to seek out the killer and carry out the requirements of Genesis 9:6. In Old Testament retributive justice, thieves are required to repay what they have stolen with interest, and killers, who cannot repay the life they have taken, must forfeit their own. But unintentional killers had one possibility to escape the avenger of blood. If they fled to one of the cities in Israel designated 'cities of refuge' and made themselves known to the city authorities, they were safe from the avenger of blood for as long as they stayed in that city. If the avenger of blood ever found the guilty party outside a city of refuge, he could instantly exact capital punishment within the law (Deuteronomy 19:1–13).

This may seem harsh to us, since the unintentional killer is effectively sentenced to life imprisonment within the limits of a city of refuge. But the purpose of the legislation was to show three things: first, that God counts human life as exceedingly precious; secondly, that God's justice is not without mercy; and thirdly, that sensible people should take all steps they possibly can to prevent accidents.

It is the last point that is of special relevance to us here. The example of unintentional killing given in the law is of an accident at work: 'a man may go into the forest with his neighbour to cut wood, and as he swings his axe to fell a tree, the head may fly off and hit his neighbour and kill him' (Deuteronomy 19:5).

In this case the killer had no malice aforethought. But it is not clear that he is without guilt. If he had taken the trouble to keep his tools in good order and check them regularly, and if the workers had taken sensible precautions, it is probable that the accident would not have happened. It is not enough to have no intention to murder anyone; we must actively seek not to put others at risk: 'Do not do anything that endangers your neighbour's life. I am the LORD' (Leviticus 19:16).

The Lord himself watches over our actions, our hearts and all events that befall. We must be tireless in seeking the welfare of those around us, and not simply looking after Number One.

This principle should guide us as we interact with other computer users. It is not enough to stop short of deliberately destroying someone else's data. We must actively avoid endangering their data. In our highly networked and technology dependent world, damage to data can have real and tragic consequences. Accidents will happen. But we can try to make sure they do not happen to our neighbours in cyberspace because of our selfish or careless actions.

Here are some practical principles which, if applied, should help to minimize the risks of our computer use to others in cyberspace.

1. Do not access other people's computer system or private files without their permission. (Don't trespass.)

2. Do not try to find out information about other people's computer systems without their permission. (Don't try to discover what's none of your business.)

3. Install anti-virus software on your computer, and keep it up to date. (Don't be responsible for passing viruses on to your friends.)

4. Regularly install operating system and application security upgrade patches provided by your software manufacturer. (Don't make things easy for hackers and virus writers.)

5. Never forward chain emails, virus warnings or spam postings. (Don't be a well-meaning nuisance.)

We shall not go far wrong in this area if we subject all our behaviour to the commands of Jesus: 'In everything, do to others what you would have them do to you' (Matthew 7:12), and 'Love your neighbour as yourself' (Luke 10:27, quoting Leviticus 19:18).

Blood lust

So much for the accidental damage we can inflict on other people's property, on their peace of mind, or even on their lives, by irresponsible computer use. But the Sixth Commandment goes further than just warning us to be careful. It is a prohibition on *murder*, and murder has its source in the rage and hatred of the human heart. Are there any ways in which our use of computer technology can reinforce or inflame these deep, dark, destructive passions?

The last decade has seen the appearance of graphically vivid, extremely violent video games. In the game *Mortal Kombat*, players are encouraged to decapitate, disembowel or otherwise butcher their opponents. Is it possible to 'play' at being a violent killer in the context of fast-paced, total-immersion simulation, and then walk away mentally or morally unscathed? While games manufacturers deny any connection between violence in cyberspace and violence in the real world, many researchers, parents and games players are deeply concerned.

Analysis carried out after the American Civil War (1861–65) found that only 15%–20% of infantry soldiers could bring themselves to fire on an exposed enemy soldier. Understandably, this shocked US military leaders, who set out to devise training methods that would increase the readiness of soldiers to kill. In this they were extremely successful, as research found that, by the time of the Korean War (1950–53), 55% of soldiers were willing to shoot to kill, and by Vietnam (1956–75) the figure had risen to more than 90%. One of the most successful training techniques was 'operant conditioning', in which trainees were repeatedly placed in simulated situations in which they learned to fire on reflex at dummy targets. Lt. Col. David Grossman spent his career in the US Army as an expert in 'killology', the psychology of killing. He is troubled by the potential impact of violent video games:

> ... soldiers learn to fire at realistic, man-shaped sil-houettes that pop into their field of view. That is the stimulus. The trainees have only a split second to engage the target. The conditioned response is to shoot the target, and then it drops. Stimulus-response, stimulus-response, stimulus-response – soldiers or police officers experience hundreds of repetitions. Later, when soldiers are on the battlefield or a police officer is walking a beat and somebody pops up with a gun, they will shoot reflexively and shoot to kill. We know that 75–80 percent of the shooting on the modern battlefield is the result of this kind of stimulus-response training.
>
> Now, if you're a little troubled by that, how much more should we be troubled by the fact that every time a child plays an interactive point-and-shoot video game, he is learning the exact same conditioned reflex and motor skills.[12]

'Games that focus on killing raise kids who think it is OK to kill,' says Mervin Stoltzfus, Director of the campaigning group Christian Peacemaker Teams.[13] Anecdotes are often produced to support such claims, such as the fact that Eric Harris and Dylan Klebold, who carried out the fatal shooting of fifteen people at Columbine High School in the USA in 1999, were hooked on the violent role-playing game *Doom*. Beyond anecdote, however, the results of academic research point in the same direction. For example, a Japanese research group led by Professor Ryuta Kawashima has shown that prolonged video-game playing leads to understimulation of the frontal lobe, which is linked to learning, memory and emotional problems. Professor Kawashima believes that society will get more violent as the new generation of game-playing children gets older. He says, 'The importance of this discovery cannot be underestimated and the implications are very serious.'[14] Arnold Goldstein, Director of the Center for Research in Aggression at the University of Syracuse, agrees: 'Playing with war toys legitimizes and makes violent behaviour acceptable.'[15]

Killology expert David Grossman draws an uncomfortable historical parallel: 'We have raised a generation of barbarians who have learned to associate violence with pleasure, like Romans cheering and snacking as the Christians were slaughtered in the Colosseum.'[16]

Why should we choose to fill our minds and condition our reflexes with visions of extreme violence? We are *God's* people, called to love and peace, not hatred and violence. We dare not toy with slaughter, lest we get a taste for it, and become like moral Draculas, who yearn for regular feasts of blood.

Our thought lives are important. Our habitual thoughts will shape our future thinking. If we dwell indulgently on our lusts for violence or for sex (see chapter 7) or whatever, and fill our eyes and our hearts with damaging images, we risk awakening our demons in both the psychological and the theological senses. 'Flee the evil desires of youth,' says Paul, 'and pursue righteousness, faith, love and peace' (2 Timothy 2:22). 'Resist the devil and he will flee from you,' says James (James 4:7).

Paul's advice for cultivating a wholesome and godly thought life is not just to avoid thinking bad thoughts; it is deliberately and consciously to choose to think good thoughts: 'whatever is true, whatever is noble, whatever is right, whatever is pure, whatever is lovely, whatever is admirable – if anything is excellent or praiseworthy – think about such things' (Philippians 4:8).

So let's not waste our time investing our ingenuity and twisting our hearts by planning how we can violate system security or kill the monster to get to the next level of a game that leads us nowhere worth going. Instead, let's match up our thoughts and our deeds with God's as we put the Sixth Net Commandment into practice:

The Sixth Net Commandment

Do not play with violence or act irresponsibly
towards others in cyberspace.

Prayer

Lord, you know every heart. You know that I habitually put
myself first, and often disregard the needs of others. Please
forgive me for my sins of carelessness, thoughtlessness or deliber--
ate malice towards others.

[Confess any specific matters on your conscience.]

Lord, please help me as a computer user to treat others with
the love and dignity I have been shown by Jesus. Help me to love
as Jesus loves. Deliver me from accidentally damaging other
people's property, and help me to remain vigilant so I can help
and not hinder other computer users.

[If you are hooked on violent computer games, add this section.]

And Lord, please deliver me from an unhealthy attachment to
violent computer games. Forgive me for the time I have wasted,
and deliver me from the hatred I have invested in. Please break
the addictive power of these games in my life, and help me to
replace them with something more constructive for your
kingdom.

In Jesus' name. Amen.

chapter 7

Let's talk about sex

You shall not commit adultery.
(Exodus 20:14)

The hour was late and the night was cold as I searched in vain for my hotel. The directions I had been given seemed incomplete or just plain wrong as I scoured the area to the north of the Arc de Triomphe in Paris. After I passed the same man for the third time, he stepped forward, glanced cautiously around, and, in a barely audible voice, enquired, 'You want to see some girls, Monsieur?'

Disgusted to be propositioned like this, I stomped off in search of my hotel. Ten frustrating minutes later I found myself in the same spot, beside the same man.

'Lovely girls. You want to see them?'

Certainly not! I headed off in another direction.

This time it took just five minutes to wind up back beside the man. Stepping out of the shadows and wrapping his regulation dirty raincoat tighter about him, he sighed, 'Monsieur, you are obviously lost. What are you looking for?'

I told him the name of my hotel.

'*Tiens!* No-one can ever find that one. Follow me; I'll take you there.'

And so I was delivered to the lobby of my hotel by one of the pimps of l'Etoile, to the evident disapproval of the concierge.

Anyone who wanders round the Internet for long enough is sure to bump into the online equivalent of that man in his grubby raincoat. You're searching for something completely unrelated when forward will step the online pimp with his brazen offer: 'You want to see some girls?'

The only wise response to such a proposition is a firm 'No'. But for many this turns out to be easier in theory than in practice. We are, after all, sexual beings with sexual appetites. The first command in the Bible affirms our sexuality: 'Be fruitful and increase in number' (Genesis 1:28). This is more than a command; it's a blessing, and most people rightly see sex in this way. But the very strength of our sexual appetites makes us vulnerable to exploitation by those who see a way of channelling our desires for their own ends.

Online turn-on

The basis of all commerce is supply and demand. Whoever can supply the demands of the market at a price the market will bear stands to make money. Those who find a way to stimulate additional demand will see their fortunes increasing. People in business need to examine themselves regularly to see whether there is anything they would *not* do to achieve business success, because finding a human weakness and exploiting it is one of the surest routes to commercial profit – and to moral ruin.

In 1979 Gerard van der Leun, President of The Source (one of the first Internet service providers), observed in *Wired* magazine: 'All media, if they are to get a jump-start in the market and become successful, must address themselves to mass drives – those things we hold in common as basic human needs. But of all these: food, shelter, sex and money; sex is the one drive that can elicit immediate consumer response.'

The accuracy of van der Leun's insight can now be seen, as he has proved to be exactly correct in the case of Internet technologies: 'Porn merchants have been the creative pioneers of e-commerce. They were the first to use shopping-cart technology and credit cards for online payment. They figured out ways to transmit large graphic files despite narrow bandwidth. And they were early adopters of innovations such as streaming video.'[1]

Estimates of the size of the Internet pornography industry vary from about $1.5 to $4 billion. Even if it's at the lower end of the range, that's an awful lot of money. Since so much is at stake, online pornographers have poured enormous reserves of ingenuity – and hard cash – into marketing their product. It is in their interests to increase their market size, both by encouraging existing consumers to consume more, and by attracting more first-time buyers. They use the same tactics to go after both groups: keep reminding people of the allure and easy availability of the product. Clever design in X-rated websites ensures that search engines drive as many visitors there as possible. You may be searching for something innocent and unrelated when suddenly there's the proposition and the opportunity: 'You want to see some girls?' Or you may open that unsolicited email to find the same offer: 'You want to see some girls?' (If your preference is guys you can be sure you will not be overlooked by the pornographers.)

For many of us the honest reflex answer is, 'Of course I want to see them!' The pornographers' blandishments hit us – if you'll pardon the expression – below the belt, addressing our primal desires rather than our rational or moral judgment. They are carefully targeted to find our point of weakness and exploit it.

Some observers deny the scale of the problem. Yes, there *is* pornography on the Internet, they say; but just as you are free not to look at pornographic magazines, so you can choose not to look at pornography on the Internet. For example, professional technology-watcher Don Tapscott takes a relaxed view:

> How widespread and serious is the problem? To listen to some of the Web's critics, you would think that distributing pornography was the Web's *raison d'être*. It's not. As it turns out, pornographic images represent less than one half of one percent of images on the Net

– far less than the magazine rack at most newsstands or grocery stores.[2]

Tapscott is right to insist on getting the facts straight. Some anti-pornography campaigners *have* overstated the scale of the threat. The Internet is a useful tool which a minority of people use for exploiting the weaknesses of others, not a fundamentally wicked medium. However, Tapscott's libertarian techno-optimism makes him more accepting of the risks than may be wise. For example, he approvingly quotes the following comment from Reanna Alder, a fifteen-year-old Internet user: 'I have never "stumbled" into a site I didn't want to see. Not like on TV where I have occasionally flicked the channel only to "stumble" into some gruesome murder scene.'[3]

I'm happy for Reanna that she has so far escaped accidental encounter with the dark side of the Internet. I wish I could say the same, and I know I am not alone. I have visited several innocent-sounding websites only to find explicit portrayals of sex acts in vivid colour. Or perhaps the content of the site is as advertised, but suddenly a rush of other browser windows pops up on the screen, each catering for a slightly different sexual preference. For every window you kill, it seems as if two more appear, so it can take some time to clear your screen of lurid images.

Pornographers have a product to promote; they are not sitting around waiting for us to find them. They're out looking for us. The potential profits provide a powerful incentive to use every marketing trick in the book to attract new customers by offering free samples. Like drug dealers, they offer the first fix for nothing to create the demand they will gladly supply for a fee in future. Whether by disguising their tasters as *bona fide* information websites, or by email targeting, they are coming after us in search of our weaknesses.

Leaving aside those who renounce the Internet because it can be abused, and those who enthusiastically embrace the abuses, there has been a variety of responses to the existence of unwholesome material on the Net. An increasing number of Internet service providers actively police the sites they host, closing down any that fail to comply with their 'decency' code. Some search-engine operators have a similar policy, and those that don't may offer a 'family filter' which automatically rejects sites deemed offensive. Users may also invest in filter programs such as CyberPatrol, SurfWatch or Net Nanny for their own PCs to help deflect as much offensive material as possible.

Taking these steps can certainly hold back a substantial part of the flood of disturbing material on the Net, but none of them is perfect and the price of using them is that they are bound to block some wholesome material that gets inadvertently caught in their filters. (Consider, for example, the challenges of researching this chapter with filtering software in place!) Many people judge the irritations of filtering software a price worth paying to protect themselves and their children from deliberate exploitation by the Net pimps with their cynical agenda of emotional entrapment. But since the protection can never be 100%, we cannot rely on the technology to protect us. We must work out our values – preferably before exposure to temptation – and then live by them.

Lust of the eyes

Is pornography really so bad? After all, the human body is God's handiwork. Adam and Eve were naked and unashamed in Eden (Genesis 3:7).

Nakedness and pornography are not the same thing. Nakedness is simply an absence of clothing, and can be highly unerotic. In many societies nakedness or semi-nakedness is a part of normal life. Pornography, by contrast, is the deliberate composition of visual images so as to stir erotic desires in the viewer.

The Bible speaks of 'the lust of the eyes' (1 John 2:16). This is what pornography feeds and exacerbates. The lust of the eyes becomes the lust of the heart. The compiler of the book of Proverbs includes a scene in which a beautiful prostitute seduces a simple young man.

> I noticed among the young men
> a youth who lacked judgment.
> He was going down the street near [the adulteress's]
>   corner,

walking along in the direction of her house
at twilight, as the day was fading,
as the dark of night set in.

Then out came a woman to meet him,
dressed like a prostitute and with crafty intent ...
With persuasive words she led him astray;
she seduced him with her smooth talk.
All at once he followed her
like an ox going to the slaughter,
like a deer stepping into a noose
till an arrow pierces his liver,
like a bird darting into a snare,
little knowing it will cost him his life.
(Proverbs 7:7–10, 21–23)

Pornography is virtual prostitution. It uses the allure of the 'bait' to overwhelm the judgment of the prey. If pornography objectifies the models it portrays, then it also makes fools of those who succumb to its attractions. Both prostitution and pornography are dangerous to our emotional and spiritual health. If we allow our desires to rule us, we shall shrink to become no more than the sum of our desires, always hungry for more, never satisfied.

You don't have to be 'looking for it' in order to be ensnared: King David was just minding his own business when he happened to catch sight of one of the most beautiful women in Jerusalem having a bath. Instead of doing the decent thing and looking away, the king stayed around to become a Peeping Tom. Embarrassment turned to curiosity, which turned to lust. And, just like so many others before and since, the lust of the eyes set fire to the lust of the heart. It was not enough just to *look* at her beauty; he had to *possess* her sexually too.

Well, what did he expect? One thing leads to another. In this case it led to an adulterous affair, an unwanted pregnancy and ultimately the effective murder of the wronged husband. (Read the story in 2 Samuel 11:14–17.) All things considered, it would have been so much easier if David had just covered his eyes when Bathsheba dropped her towel.

Pornography is bad news. Its primary purpose for the viewer is to whet the sexual appetites, to fan the flames of lust for its own sake. 'What harm does it do to anyone?' we may ask. After all, isn't it just appreciation of the beautiful bodies the Creator has so fearfully and wonderfully made? A private porno-surfing session isn't an orgy. It's not like going to bed with someone, is it?

Yes, it is, says Jesus; it's exactly like going to bed with someone. 'You have heard that it was said, "Do not commit adultery." But I tell you that anyone who looks at a woman lustfully has already committed adultery with her in his heart' (Matthew 5:27–28).

Pornography has real moral consequences. It gives birth to sin in our hearts and grieves the heart of the Lord. John Houghton has identified ten good reasons why pornography is bad for us:

1. It divorces sexual stimulation from the intimacy of love and marriage.
2. It reduces the image of God to the level of brute creation.
3. It fosters a climate of sexual promiscuity and infidelity.
4. It exploits, degrades and denies the feelings of the participants.
5. It feeds on greed to induce addiction and obsession.
6. It nurtures spiritual hardness, anger and aggression.
7. It furthers social isolation and self-centred introversion.
8. It saps our creative energies and stunts the higher emotions.
9. It encourages hypocrisy and secretive lust in personal relationships.
10. It swamps the imagination with crude images to the exclusion of the finer.[4]

Talking dirty

Ogling naughty pictures on screen isn't the only way to stray into dangerous sexual territory in cyberspace. At least part of the popularity of one of the most popular applications, online chat, may be the ease with which it can turn into online chat-up, or even old-fashioned (though now technologically mediated) 'talking dirty'.

> Sex on the Net goes far beyond the pornographic images that blanket the Web. Porn has been around for millennia and the Internet has merely increased its scope and availability. The real change brought by the Net is the innovation in sexual conversation between real people typing at different machines; this is the most potent side of the new sexual revolution, created by the crossing of our animal drives with one of the most powerful communication technologies ever invented. This interaction is at the core of what is becoming known among a growing circle of psychologists as the crack cocaine of sex addiction.[5]

The comparison with hard drugs sounds alarming, but is not inappropriate.

> According to a study done by Al Cooper, a psychologist at Stanford, one percent of all Internet users can be classified as 'cybersex compulsives,' those whose sexual Internet use is enough to lead to negative consequences at home and at work; another eight percent of all users … spend more than 11 hours a week pursuing online sex.[6]

According to Robert Weiss, Director of the Sexual Recovery Institute in Los Angeles,

> Sex addiction is not about sex. It is not about orgasm … It's about looking for sex. Your heart is racing. Your

endorphins are pumping. You are in a drug-induced narcotic state.

This narcosis is not an exclusively male problem. The Director of the Center for Online Addiction, Dr Kimberley Young, claims that though men seem to be generally more 'hard-wired' to like pornography (i.e. more susceptible to its temptations) than women, Internet chat rooms 'become a safe forum for women. And they can find it addictive to explore sexuality in different ways.'

As with drugs, alcohol or gambling, the addictive grip of Internet chat is felt not just by 'losers' who have nothing else to live for, but in people across all ages and social groups. Addicts don't set out to become addicted; they typically stumble into patterns of behaviour that start innocently enough and gradually lead to the point where the individual's own moral boundaries are crossed, with an associated loss of will and ability to stop.

For example, in late 1999 the Bishop-elect of a western US Episcopalian diocese had to step down after admitting that he had 'engaged in inappropriate e-mail exchanges with four women over the past two years'. The exchanges had contained 'unacceptable "endearments" and "romantic" allusions'.[7]

Why would a senior churchman risk his faith, his job, his family and his social standing by getting involved in such behaviour? No-one plans to fall so spectacularly, but, as this example shows, it is all too possible to drift into conducting online conversations we would never dream of having face to face. Perhaps it is the anonymity that makes it so easy – the fact that obscene comments can be exchanged without having to look another person in the eyes. Without the constraint of visible eye-contact, perhaps we more readily forget that the Lord's eyes are always upon us.

What is certain is that sexually oriented chat is astonishingly widespread. The journalist Nicholas Thompson set out to investigate the phenomenon in the chat rooms hosted by America On Line (AOL). No doubt his experience is typical of many other online chat communities.

The public chat groups on AOL are divided into cat-
egories ... They range from general meeting places to
discussions about rock stars to rooms for cross-
dressers. But in almost all of them, users mainly flirt or
talk about sex. The chat rooms aren't much more than
a sprawling singles bar with sections for every sexual
fetish known to humanity – and, it often seems, a few
others that must have just been dreamed up.

Researching this ... I put in dozens of room hours,
saving conversations on my hard drive. On five separate evenings I logged chat rooms for the entire night
and found that at least two-thirds of the chat is
flirtatious or sex-related.[8]

In my own Internet use, I have found the following to be a
useful principle: *Only engage in Internet chat for the purpose of
obtaining or imparting factual information.* Thus, chat rooms that
exist to act as 'knowledge exchanges' among enthusiasts for a
particular model of car, software program, regional cuisine, or
whatever, can be invaluable sources of obscure, but useful, information. But, in my experience, chat rooms that offer less focused
'chat' tend to be at best a waste of time, and more usually degrade
into coarse and seedy nastiness.

This raises the question of why anyone should actually want to
stay shut away in a room having a typed 'conversation' about
nothing much with complete strangers. It makes just about as
much sense as staying shut away alone in a room taking drugs to
find 'happiness'. The tragedy of both is that those who get caught
up in the addiction come to see their fix as that which makes life
meaningful, when in fact they have actually opted *out of* life in
favour of a pale imitation.

After his marathon session investigating chat rooms, Nicholas
Thompson concluded:

The Internet provides an illusion of attractiveness, of
intimacy, and of self-confidence. It allows you to have
a relationship or an affair without having to get to

really know the person you're with; and it lets you end the relationship just by pressing the delete key. It allows you to become blond or honest by simply saying you are. It allows you to play the role of [a playboy] without having to wake up in a strange bed with a hangover. On the Internet, we can all live Life Lite. And when that happens, it becomes impossible to access the complexities of relationships that really make them worthwhile.[9]

Overcome evil with good

One of the characters in the romantic drama we call the Song of Songs has this warning for us: 'Do not arouse or awaken love until it so desires' (Song 3:5). In a dramatic work that celebrates human love as a gift from God and a signpost to the love of God, it is a reminder that the passions of the heart run deep, and are not to be trifled with. We are capable of experiencing both noble and wicked desires, so we must exercise moral judgment in deciding what to do with them. If we simply gratify every desire that arises within us, the moment will come when we shall no longer be able to control our desires; they will control us.

In a solemn passage at the start of the letter to the Romans, Paul describes how people can repeatedly choose pleasure-seeking self-indulgence until it becomes such a habit of life that they lose the ability to choose at all, and find themselves locked into self-destructive, godless patterns of life. The horror of this is that God finally affirms rebels in their rebellion. We make our bed, and God sorrowfully allows us to lie in it. Three times Paul uses the chilling phrase, 'God gave them over ...': '*God gave them over* in the sinful desires of their hearts to sexual impurity for the degrading of their bodies with one another ... *God gave them over* to shameful lusts ... *he [God] gave them over* to a depraved mind, to do what ought not to be done' (Romans 1:24, 26, 28, italics added).

No wonder Paul elsewhere writes so eloquently on how to overcome our primal desires. Writing to Titus, he outlines the content of a basic Christian education programme. Older men need to be instructed in various subjects, including *self-control.* Women, both young and old, must be taught, among other things, the need for *self-control.* And the main subject in the syllabus for young men is – you've guessed it – *self-control* (Titus 2:1–6).

Paul is offering us much more than an early version of the 'Just say no' slogan. Human weakness and the realities of addiction make just saying 'no' something that can seem beyond our power. Paul himself gives us the clearest picture of the moral struggle that rages inside the human heart: 'I have the desire to do what is good, but I cannot carry it out. For what I do is not the good I want to do; no, the evil I do not want to do – this I keep on doing' (Romans 7:15, 18–19).

Is the dilemma hopeless? Mercifully not, for what we are powerless to do by ourselves, God has made possible through his grace. First, he gives us his Spirit to live in us to enable us to overcome even these primal impulses to do evil. Secondly, he offers us his amazing forgiveness, so that we need not be locked into a downward spiral in which we get so depressed by our past failures that we cannot muster the will to live right going forward. Thirdly, he motivates us with a morality based on love, not law. When we try to be good by avoiding prohibited activities, we fail. Instead, he enables us to live positively by finding out what pleases the Lord and putting it into action.

The 'Just say no' principle can feel terribly abstract when we are faced with a really attractive temptation. Better to follow the 'How can I express my love for Jesus?' principle moment by moment. The best defence against the allure of lust is not prohibition, but greater love. A happily married man remains faithful to his wife, not by reminding himself every day that he must not commit adultery, but because he finds the whole idea of adultery preposterous. He loves his wife so much that the thought of cheating on her and hurting her so terribly is intolerable. Likewise, in our struggle against sin, we need to find out what pleases the Lord (Ephesians 5:10), and put it into action because we love him.

For the grace of God that brings salvation has appeared to all people. It teaches us to say 'No' to ungodliness and worldly passions, and to live self-controlled, upright and godly lives in this present age, while we wait for the blessed hope – the glorious appearing of our great God and Saviour, Jesus Christ, who gave himself for us to redeem us from all wicked-ness and to purify for himself a people that are his very own, eager to do what is good (Titus 2:11–14).

In Christianity, morality is relational: we live to please our Lord and Saviour. The temptations we have explored in this chapter are temptations to play with profound human drives as if they could be explored outside of real relationships with other people and, most importantly, with God. Breaking the Seventh Commandment, 'You shall not commit adultery', may seem attractive because of the sexual adventure it promises, but the price is astronomically high: violating ourselves, the other person and (if we are married) our spouse, and grieving the heart of our Father in heaven.

In cyberspace, we find the same temptations to toy with illicit passions as if they had no relational consequences. But they do: they can devastate loved ones, twist and diminish our own hearts, and wound even our loving Lord. That's why we need to pay such careful attention to the Seventh Net Commandment:

The Seventh Net Commandment

Do not have anything to do pornography, perversion
or inappropriate relationships on the Internet.

Prayer

Loving Lord, thank you that you love me with such passion that you were willing to die to rescue me from the consequences of my lack of self-control. Thank you that you have not abandoned me, even though I have often deserved it.

[Confess any sins of lust with which you have grieved the Lord.]

Please forgive me for preferring the short-term gratification of these sins to the eternal glory of knowing you and being known by you. Please help me, day by day, to live to please you. Help me to be more motivated by the passions of your heart than by the depravity of my own. And help me to love you utterly and to honour you with a life of purity and holiness.

In Jesus' name. Amen.

You may find it helpful to use Psalm 51:1–12 as a prayer. This was composed by King David after his affair with Bathsheba was exposed.

chapter 8

Give and take

You shall not steal.
(Exodus 20:15)

Simon was a fairly ordinary fourteen-year-old schoolboy living in New Zealand. He wasn't considered by his teachers to be one of the school's high achievers. He was just a regular kid.

When the Union Building Society in Simon's home town installed a gleaming new cash machine or ATM in their branch, it naturally aroused the curiosity of locals. It was the early 1980s, when ATMs were still new technology. Time passed, and the ATM became part of everyday life. Lots of people started to use it to withdraw and deposit cash. Simon applied for an ATM card, and soon he was using it too.

One day, Simon had an idea. It wasn't that he wanted to cause trouble, it was just that he was curious. He cut up an old breakfast-cereal packet and put the pieces in a deposit envelope. Then he went to the ATM and informed it that he wanted to deposit some money. It instructed him: 'Please key the sum you wish to deposit, followed by ENTER.'

Simon thought for a moment, and then he typed, '1000000<ENTER>'.

One million NZ dollars! Surely the system wouldn't allow that much money to be entered through a hole-in-the-wall machine? Even supposing he used high-denomination notes, a million dollars would never fit in a deposit envelope. A suitcase or a wheelbarrow perhaps, but not an envelope!

'Please insert cash in one of the envelopes provided and place it in the drawer marked DEPOSIT.'

Tentatively, Simon inserted his envelope full of cardboard into the machine, and saw it disappear. That wasn't what he'd expected to happen! He took off quickly before anyone came out of the building society to see who was messing about with their ATM.

A few days later, Simon went back to the branch to check his account. To his astonishment, his balance was $1 million healthier than the last time he'd seen it. Worried that he was going to get into trouble, he withdrew $10 to see what would happen.

Several days passed. The phone didn't ring. Police officers didn't kick his door down. Amazingly, he'd succeeded in swapping an old cereal packet for $1 million! He withdrew $500, but then he had an attack of nerves and deposited it straight back into his account.

A few days later he withdrew $1,500. Once again, his conscience got the better of him, but this time he told the story to one of his teachers. The teacher took him down to the building society, where he confessed the whole sequence of events to the manager.[1]

Computer theft

Simon was guilty of committing a computer crime. It wasn't a premeditated attempt to obtain money dishonestly, though that was the end result. For him it was just a piece of teenage mischief, an experiment that went badly wrong. Unlike most high-tech robbers, he returned the loot voluntarily.

Simon's experience shows just how easy it can be to get rich quick in cyberspace. Most computer thieves are not hardened criminals who hatch their plots in smoke-filled rooms. They're opportunists who happen to be in the right place at the right time to spot a weakness in the security of a computer system, which they then exploit to their advantage.

Conventional bank robbery is a difficult and dangerous business. There are physical barriers between the would-be robber and the coveted cash: counter screens, locked doors, strong-rooms and safes. There are video cameras, security systems, burglar alarms and guards. Then there's the danger of leaving physical evidence at the scene of the crime: fingerprints, fibres from clothing, even DNA. And how about the getaway? Fleeing from the scene of the crime as quickly as possible while encumbered with the weight of stolen money? No thanks! As if all that weren't enough, in some parts of the world, escaping bank robbers are considered fair game to be shot at.

No wonder most people conclude it isn't worth the risk, even if they have no scruples about taking someone else's money.

But what if you were walking by yourself in the country and you stumbled upon a fortune in used notes? There would be no witnesses and almost no chance of being found out if you took it. What would you do? You don't know who it belongs to, but you know it isn't yours. Would you take it anyway?

That's the dilemma most computer criminals face. They're just going about their normal business when they stumble upon a way of helping themselves to a lot of money. They can execute the entire heist from the comfort and safety of a computer terminal. The sums of money that can be netted make most bank-robbery hauls look like pocket money. And the beauty of it is that most of the action takes place in cyberspace, so even if you leave loads of clues at the scene of the crime, all they will tell the police is that *someone* was responsible. It will be almost impossible to pin the blame on you. Even if you are the prime suspect, most financial institutions will be terrified of adverse publicity about their security procedures, so they probably won't press charges.

You're in a position to carry out the perfect crime and join the ranks of the super-rich. This is where the reality of your Christian faith gets put to the test. If it's simply a matter of pious words and social conventions, you'll probably take the money and run. But if you have truly become an obedient and loving servant of the

Lord Jesus Christ, you'll have strong motivation to stand firm against the temptation.

Opportunity knocks

Perhaps the whole topic of computer crime seems rather remote. You don't expect ever to face the temptation to dip your fingers into the electronic till. It's something that concerns other people, not you.

I expect that's what computer consultant Stanley Mark Rifkin thought before he stumbled upon the Security Pacific National Bank's EFT codes while working in the wire transfer room of a New York branch of the bank.

EFT, or Electronic Funds Transfer, is the system by which financial institutions move money around the world. It is difficult to say exactly how much money is transferred each day by this method, but estimates suggest that the amount handled by New York's banks alone runs into hundreds of billions of dollars. EFT is only as secure as the electronic codes used to authenticate transactions. If the codes fall into the wrong hands, bogus transactions can easily be carried out.

Unexpectedly in possession of the keys to fabulous wealth, Stanley Rifkin succumbed to temptation. Posing as a bank manager, on several occasions he telephoned a branch of the bank in Los Angeles, each time using the security codes to transfer sums of less than $1 million to a New York bank. In this way he built up a nest-egg of $10.2 million. This he transferred to a Swiss bank account. Next, he flew to Switzerland, where he withdrew the money and used it to buy diamonds, which he brought back with him into the United States.

Rifkin had committed the perfect crime. The chances of his ever being caught were minuscule. There was nothing to link him to the missing money, except a voice on the telephone. So confident was he of his untouchability that he boasted openly about what he had done, and it was this that led to his eventual arrest and conviction.

Vast sums have been lost through EFT fraud. In 1988 an amount variously reported to be between $33 million and $54 million was illegally transferred from a branch of the Union Bank of Switzerland in London to a private bank account in the small town of Nyon, near Lausanne. The theft came to light only because a computer failure at the bank in Nyon meant that all EFT transactions had to be processed by hand that day.[2]

In May 1988, seven people were arrested in New York after trying to transfer $70 million out of the accounts of Brown-Forman, Merrill Lynch and United Airlines at the First National Bank of Chicago. The crime was detected only when the Merrill Lynch account became overdrawn. Likewise, five men were arrested in July 1989 after trying to transfer $90 million from Swedish banks to Gibraltar, using the SWIFT banking network.[3]

Probably the largest EFT fraud to date took place in 1984, when around $260 million disappeared from the finances of the Volkswagen company in West Germany. The perpetrator was never found, though a number of senior Volkswagen employees were sacked or suspended.

The vast majority of computer thieves are first-time offenders. According to a major UK study, 25% of offenders are managers or supervisors, and 24% are specialist IT staff, but a surprisingly high 31% are clerks or cashiers with few technical skills. In the words of the study's author: 'Not many crimes ... demonstrate high technical ingenuity on the part of the perpetrator. Most exhibit an opportunistic exploitation of an inherent weakness in the computer system being used.'[4]

According to computer crime expert Leslie Ball, computer criminals 'tend to be relatively honest and in a position of trust; few would do anything to harm another human, and most do not consider their crime to be truly dishonest'.[5] Another researcher in the field, Hugo Cornwall, claims that one of the more troubling aspects of the phenomenon is how 'nice suburban people with jobs that give them access to sensitive information, systems and data are able to justify to themselves and their friends the committing of certain types of criminal act'.[6]

If you are a 'nice', 'relatively honest' person working in a position of trust, and if you have access to computer information systems, then the next person to be tempted could be you.

How to commit a computer crime

Apart from discovering and wrongfully using EFT codes, there are many other ways of perpetrating large-scale theft using computers. We shall briefly consider a few of these here – not to suggest ideas for the creative criminal to pursue, but rather so that ordinary readers can appreciate the manifold forms computer crime can take.

In the *resting money* method, the perpetrator (normally the employee of a financial institution) arranges for large sums of money in transit between accounts to rest for short periods of time in his or her own account. This gives the account a hefty average balance, on which interest may be earned.

In the *rounding-error collection* method, the fractions of a penny or cent that may be produced during calculations are credited to the criminal's account rather than to the originating account. The sums involved are so minute in each case that no-one is likely to notice. Where the volume of transactions is high, the value of the sum collected can grow surprisingly quickly.

The rounding-error collection method is a special case of the *salami* method, in which the criminal collects a large sum through shaving trivial cuts off numerous different accounts, like so many slices of salami. For example, a substantial fortune could be amassed by trimming a few pennies off all the accounts held by a bank. In case of discovery, it looks like a simple instance of computer error involving insignificant amounts. But, as the proverb says, 'If you look after the pennies, the pounds will look after themselves.'

In the *Trojan horse* method, false information is inserted into the system, causing it to act in ways that profit the perpetrator. For example, a cheque-writing program could be fed an augmented list of cheque requests for fictitious creditors. These can later be collected and cashed by the criminal.

The *inactive accounts* method takes advantage of the fact that every organization that maintains customer accounts will have a certain number of long-inactive accounts on its books at any time. These exist for a variety of reasons, including change in financial circumstances, illness, death, or simply forgetfulness on the part of the account holder. An employee with access to the account activity list can identify those accounts that have been inactive for the longest time, and then empty them of funds.

Beyond the financial sector

Computer crime is not confined to the upper echelons of the financial sector. In a society that relies as heavily as ours on computers for all its affairs, it is becoming an option for citizens in just about every walk of life.

Computer crime doesn't even have to involve money. Jerry Schneider, an eighteen-year-old student in the USA, gained access to information about Pacific Telephone's security procedures by posing as a magazine reporter researching a story about their parts-distribution system. He found out that part requests were logged by touch-tone telephone, and then delivered to whatever address was requested. He also worked out a way of convincing the computer system that supported the whole operation that his requests were *bona fide* internal orders. In this way Schneider was able to collect vast quantities of telephone equipment using a few designated pick-up points. These he resold through a telecommunications company he set up for the purpose. He was eventually caught following a tip-off to the police from one of his ten employees. By then, over a million dollars'-worth of telephone equipment had been misappropriated.

Since the dawn of human social organization, civil servants working in local and national government have had to come to terms with the seductions of corruption. Gifted public servants have always been, and probably always will be, less well paid than their peers in the private sector. An understandable sense of injustice may grow, and from this a determination to put the injustice right by taking what is 'rightfully mine'. The end is used to justify the means, and a crime is committed. The particular tension that makes crime so ready an option in public service is that individuals without much personal wealth nevertheless possess a great deal of professional power. The awarding of contracts can be influenced – for a consideration. The progress of planning applications can be obstructed or facilitated – for a consideration. Large sums of tax revenue have to be collected and managed – and can be misappropriated.

Public service is an honourable calling, and most public servants carry out their tasks with diligence and honesty out of a sense of the value of contributing to the smooth running of society. The Bible presents ample positive models of faithful believers in government service, including Joseph (Genesis 41:41–57), Daniel (2:48–49) and Nehemiah (5:14–16). Cheap stereotypes, such as 'the bent civil servant', benefit no-one, and actually insult and misrepresent the profession. This said, it is important to acknowledge that public service can offer powerful temptations to cross ethical lines, and this is borne out by a steady trickle of convictions in the courts.

The National Audit Office uncovered a series of computer thefts by British civil servants in 1991.[7] The litany of wrongdoing was shameful. Inland Revenue staff had arranged for their friends' tax codes to be altered favourably. Post Office staff had helped themselves to funds in inactive accounts. Ministry of Defence staff had used computers to redirect government equipment to other beneficiaries. Driver and Vehicle Licensing Agency staff had instructed computer systems to issue false driving licences. Department of Employment staff had arranged for benefit cheques to be sent to false addresses so they could collect and cash them.

Victimless crime?

Some people try to justify computer crime – at least to themselves – by claiming that it is 'victimless'. It is not individuals who suffer, but organizations. Perhaps in some cases no-one suffers at all.

Let's be absolutely clear about this: there can be no such thing as a victimless crime. Somebody always has to pay.

Just because the victims' faces cannot be seen or their names known, they do not cease to be victims. Where money is stolen from the Social Security budget, less is left behind to feed the hungry, to clothe the needy and to house the homeless. When it is taken from the bank accounts of big business, it leaves companies less able to create new jobs and more likely to cut existing jobs. It means less return for private shareholders, and less return for institutional shareholders such as pension funds. This leads ultimately to reduced weekly income for pensioners. Theft is also a business cost, which gets passed on to customers. Ultimately, innocent customers pay for the dishonesty of a few.

Where funds are stolen from banks, the loss has to be borne by somebody. It may be the bank's customers, through increased rates of interest on borrowing or increased account administration charges. It may be the bank's shareholders through reduced dividends. The same practical consequences follow even in salami-slicing swindles. Either very many private individuals are having tiny sums stolen from them, or the bank is having a large sum stolen from it in numerous wafer-thin slices. The reality of the theft and of its consequent creation of victims is obvious in the latter case, but how about in the former?

It is true that every customer of the bank who has a fraction of a penny (or whatever the thickness of the salami slice may be) removed from their account has not lost a significant amount financially. They are unlikely to be plunged into destitution as a result of the loss. But the scale of the loss is not the only issue. Each private individual's property rights have been violated. Unlike Marxism, which holds that 'property is theft', the Bible insists that each individual is entitled to hold property, but that it must be held, not in absolute ownership, but in trust for God as his steward. Thus theft violates the individual's property rights; it affronts the dignity of the individual, however small the sum taken. But it also affronts the Lord God, who is the ultimate owner of all things.

All we have comes to us by God's grace. When we steal, we don't just deprive other people of the blessing God has given them; we also affirm that we are prepared to work at cross-purposes with God to get our hands on the things we want. The Lord's instruction in the Eighth Commandment is unambiguous: 'You shall not steal.' Attempts to get around the clarity of the prohibition by asserting that computer theft is not theft at all, because it is victimless, are hopelessly forlorn. In most cases the human victims are obvious, given a moment's thought. In all cases, theft is an offence against God, the ultimate owner of everything. And in all cases, the computer thief is a victim of his or her own sinfulness.

The Old Testament story of Achan starkly illustrates how theft inevitably harms the thief (Joshua 5:13 – 7:26). The Lord had instructed Joshua and the Israelites how they should capture the city of Jericho. It would not be a conventional military manoeuvre. Instead, the Israelites should go out and march round Jericho once a day, for six days, with the priests sounding their trumpets. On the seventh day, they should march round the city seven times. Then the priests should give a long blast and the people must shout with all their might. When the Israelites did as the Lord commanded and raised a great shout, the walls of the city collapsed and the Israelites were able to take it.

There could be no mistaking the divine intervention that delivered the city into the hands of Joshua and the people. Everyone understood: the plunder from the city belonged to the victor, and in this case the victor was the Lord God himself. 'They burned the whole city and everything in it, but they put the silver and gold and the articles of bronze and iron into the treasury of the LORD's house' (Joshua 6:24).

In their next battle, however, when the Israelites went out against the city of Ai, victory proved elusive. When Joshua asked the Lord why they had failed, he was told that victory would continue to elude them until the goods that were rightfully God's were returned to him. Joshua assembled all the people and, through a very public process of elimination (Joshua 6:16–18), the Lord identified Achan as the culprit.

> Joshua said to Achan, 'Tell me what you have done; do not hide it from me.'
> Achan replied, 'It is true! I have sinned against the LORD, the God of Israel. This is what I have done: When I saw in the plunder a beautiful robe from Babylonia, two hundred shekels of silver and a wedge

of gold weighing fifty shekels, I coveted them and took them. They are hidden in the ground inside my tent ...' (Joshua 7:20–21).

Achan had thought that his was a victimless crime – a crime that simply relocated these desirable items from the treasury of the Lord's house to a location where he could enjoy them better. Why should this bother God? After all, God is Lord of the whole earth, including Achan's tent. But by his selfish actions, Achan obstructed God's blessing to the entire people, and he brought down judgment on himself. He was taken outside the camp and stoned to death.

There is no such thing as a victimless crime.

Software piracy

So far, we have considered large-scale computer crime, but there is a much more widespread and logistically simple form of computer crime: software piracy. It is notoriously difficult to protect expensive software from simply being copied and distributed freely.

The total world market for software is over $100 billion per year. The US-based Software Publishers' Association estimates that, in the US alone, the cost of software piracy is in the region of $12 billion per year. According to the Lotus Corporation, over half of all potential sales of its 1–2–3 spreadsheet package have been lost to pirates. Over half!

The US-based Business Software Alliance (BSA) estimates that 40% of all software packages sold in the US are pirated. This figure rises to over 75% in Japan, Germany, Belgium, Holland and Italy. It rises further to an astonishing 80%–90% in China, Taiwan, Korea, Spain, Portugal and Switzerland.

In an earlier BSA study, it was found that 1.5 legitimate software packages were sold for every PC sold in the US. This figure fell to 0.82 in Australia, 0.65 in France and 0.4 in Italy. Do Americans use their computers for a greater range of activities than people from other nations? Possibly, but with less than half a program per computer available in Italy, it appears that a lot of people don't use their computers for anything other than decoration! There is no realistic reason to suppose that the amount of software loaded on each computer varies much between countries. It is just that attitudes to the social acceptability of software piracy differ.[8]

It is possible – even likely – that no-one who reads this book will have committed a major computer crime, though some may have been presented with opportunities, as I myself have. However, it is equally likely that a substantial proportion of readers will have been guilty of software piracy. Perhaps you are currently a software pirate. You don't think of yourself as a conventionally piratical character, living a life of conspicuous crime. You don't go through life with a great burden of guilt or worry about being found out because you've got a bootleg program on your PC.

When I ask Christians what they think about software piracy, I get four main answers.

First, 'It isn't really theft.' I don't know where people who say this think software comes from. Perhaps it just materializes on someone's disk one day, and can be freely copied from then on! Of course not. It's the result of someone's job of work. Thousands of person-years of effort may have gone into what's currently sitting on your hard disk. People had to be paid to work for all that time. Will you really steal the fruits of their labours without contributing to their wages?

Second, 'But software's so expensive!' One reason why it's expensive is that it's complicated. It's difficult to write good software; it takes time, effort and ingenuity. But a more significant reason is that not everyone pays their fair share of its cost. It would be nothing short of a scandal if ethical unbelievers ended up paying for the software Christians rip off for nothing.

Third, 'Everyone does it. Violating software copyright is the norm, so why should I be any different?' This is an appallingly bad argument for a Christian to use. It can be restated thus: 'Why shouldn't I sin? Everyone else does.' Christian morality is not defined by democratic consensus. It rests on the unchanging character of God.

Fourth, 'Software piracy is theft.' Because it is theft, it is inappropriate for Christians. It is not a victimless crime. It can, and has, put companies out of business and people out of jobs. If practised by Christians, it will tend to deaden their conscience and to lessen their awareness of the extent to which sin offends God.

Which of these four responses to software piracy do you think is biblically sustainable?

Owning up

Though some may attempt to re-categorize computer crime to prevent it from falling under the blanket prohibition of the Eighth Commandment, it should be clear that this is no more than self-justification. Any rational person, whether Christian or not, can see it for what it is. As Tom Forester and Perry Morrison assert: 'Computer crime should not present an ethical dilemma for computer professionals or computer users. Theft is theft and fraud is fraud, and both are generally accepted by our society to be morally wrong. The issues raised by computer crime are empirical and practical rather than moral.'[9]

'You shall not steal,' asserts the Eighth Commandment, with the full weight of divine authority. We can draw out the implications of this God-given rule for the world of IT as follows:

The Eighth Net Commandment

Do not steal electronic money or information,
or violate software copyright.

For some, this may be particularly hard-hitting. You know you have not followed its guidance. Perhaps you are currently benefiting from the material fruits of computer crime. It's got to stop. Jesus said: 'No servant can be a slave to two masters. Either he will hate the one and love the other, or he will be devoted to the one and despise the other. You cannot be a slave to both God and Money' (Luke 16:13). The way we apply the Eighth Commandment makes plain which of the two is our true master.

You may wish to respond that, in spite of all that's been said in this chapter, you don't think a bit of harmless software-copying really counts as grand larceny before God. After all, you still have a sense of fellowship with him. Surely, if you were doing wrong, he would have cold-shouldered you?

While it's true that the absence of a sense of fellowship with the Lord can be a valuable clue to sin in our lives, our spiritual feelings should not be relied upon naïvely. The Lord is very gracious, and may allow us to retain a sense of his nearness to facilitate our repentance – not our hardening of heart.

Judas Iscariot was a thief. As keeper of the disciples' money bag, he used to help himself to the contents (John 12:6). In spite of this, Jesus kept company with him for three years. The sinfulness of his theft was not somehow annulled by the proximity of the Lord. Rather, its toxic effect grew the longer he persisted in abusing the Lord's trust. When the day of testing came and the question 'God or money?' was posed, he chose to follow his *de facto* god: money. He 'went to the chief priests and asked, "What are you willing to give me if I hand him over to you?" So they counted out for him thirty silver coins. From then on Judas watched for an opportunity to hand him over' (Matthew 26:14–16).

The Bible has some very direct guidance for those who have broken the Eighth Commandment: 'Those who have been stealing must steal no longer, but must work, doing something useful with their own hands, that they may have something to share with those in need' (Ephesians 4:28).

It's one thing to stop stealing, but is there forgiveness for thieves? Yes, indeed – so long as there is true repentance. The Lord Jesus was crucified between two convicted robbers. One confessed and received forgiveness and eternal bliss with the Lord; the other, like Judas, despised the Lord's mercy and faced eternal separation from the Lord (Matthew 27:38; Luke 23:39–43).

Repentance is profoundly practical. More than simply being sorry, it calls for changed behaviour. First, 'those who have been stealing must steal no longer'. Secondly, where identifiable people have been affected, confession must be made and forgiveness sought (James 5:16). This may be costly, and forgiveness may be withheld. In extreme cases, it may be necessary for the due process of law to operate. If in doubt, discuss this with a more mature Christian. However appealing it may be to look good before the world, it is all-important to be justified before God, so there can be no ducking this difficult step of confession.

Thirdly, restitution should be made, where possible. As soon as Zacchaeus, the dishonest chief tax collector, encountered Jesus, he volunteered to make compensatory restitution:

> 'Look, Lord! Here and now I give half of my posses-
> sions to the poor, and if I have cheated anybody out
> of anything, I will pay back four times the amount.'
>
> Jesus said to him, 'Today salvation has come to this
> house ...' (Luke 19:8–9).

Is restitution an option for you? If you have benefited at someone else's expense through computer theft, can you pay them back with interest? It's only fair.

In the complex world of software, it can be difficult to work out how to do this in practice. Here are some down-to-earth suggestions for how to deal with software piracy.

1. Never give away or accept bootleg copies of software. Be suspicious of all distribution disks that are
   not clearly marked with the maker's identification.
2. Check the software packages on your PC to
   ascertain the legal status of each.
3. If you find any unlicensed packages that you
   seldom or never use, erase them from your system.
4. If you find any unlicensed packages that you want
   to go on using, check each package's 'Help'
   information. If it's possible to license the software
   by sending off a payment or registering via a
   website, then do so promptly. Otherwise, purchase
   a completely new version of the package from a
   legitimate source, and erase the old one.

5. Sometimes the precise status of a package may be unclear. It may be *freeware* (freely copyable, royalty-free), *shareware* (freely copyable, royalty payable) or *demoware* (freely copyable, royalty-free for a limited period, then royalty payable). If in doubt, consult the manufacturer.

Having taken all reasonable steps to ensure that your system is clear of pirated software, take a deep breath and enjoy the peace that comes from also having a conscience that's clear. It is great to be able to say, along with the writer to the Hebrews, 'We are sure that we have a clear conscience and desire to live honourably in every way' (Hebrews 13:18).

'Everyone has a price', according to the cynical old saying. Do you have a price? If so, what is it? £1,000? £100,000? £1 million? £10 million? A quarter of a billion? Or is it as little as a £10 pirated software package? 'What good is it for you to gain the whole world, yet forfeit your soul?' (Mark 8:36).

Prayer

A prayer for those who have been guilty of computer theft

Lord, I have sinned against you and done what is evil in your sight. I have taken what was not mine. I have wronged other people. And I have wronged you. Please forgive me my sins of theft. Help me to make restitution to those I have wronged. And please restore to me a good conscience, so that I may live honourably and at peace with you.

In Jesus' name. Amen.

A prayer for everyone

Lord, you are the source of all material blessing. Please help me to trust you for all that I need – my daily bread and the clothes that I wear. Help me to rely, not on my own abilities to acquire material wealth, but on you, the source of all material and spiritual wealth.

I pray this in Jesus' name. Amen.

chapter 9

Reputations

You shall not give false testimony against your neighbour.
(Exodus 20:16)

The following claim was collected on the Internet in 1998:

> The President of Procter & Gamble appeared on the
> *Phil Donahue Show* on March 1, 1994. He announced
> that, due to the openness of our society, he was
> coming out of the closet about his association with the
> Church of Satan. He stated that a large portion of his
> profits from Procter & Gamble products goes to
> support this satanic church. When asked by Donahue
> if stating this on TV would hurt his business, he
> replied, 'There are not enough Christians in the
> United States to make a difference.'

It sounds shocking, doesn't it? The President of a reputable
multinational manufacturer of leading household brands, such as
Ariel detergent, Crest toothpaste, Head and Shoulders shampoo
and Pampers nappies, claiming that a cut of our weekly shopping
bill goes directly to support the Church of Satan!

But what is even more shocking is that the claim is completely untrue. It is a slander fabricated to cause maximum damage in the marketplace to a successful, well-established company.

The lie goes back to 1980, when rumours began to circulate that Procter & Gamble was secretly controlled by the cult leader the Reverend Sun Myung Moon. Perhaps this thought was inspired by the famous Procter & Gamble 'man in the moon' trademark. Another rumour also emerged, linking the trademark to witchcraft. Shortly after that, the story about the senior Procter & Gamble executive making satanic claims on a TV talk show was added. From very early in the saga, Procter & Gamble has claimed that some distributors of its competitor, Amway Corporation, have helped to spread the rumours, and it has successfully sued six of them.[1] The rumours circulated by word of mouth for years, until they received a boost from the arrival of new communications technology. On their website, Procter & Gamble claim: 'In 1995, with the push of a button, some of Amway's top distributors used Amway's vast voice mail system to spread the rumor.'[2]

Round about this time, the Internet began to take off as a means of mass communication, and, needless to say, the rumours about Procter & Gamble developed a life of their own in cyberspace. I have received earnest warnings by email at least twice, urging me to boycott Procter & Gamble products. If the story were true, such a boycott would be reasonable; I don't want to do anything to fund Satanism. But it's a malicious lie, made all the more scandalous by the fact that those it really attacks are the ordinary people who depend on Procter & Gamble for their livelihood.

Since the rumour began to circulate, the basic slander has remained fairly stable, but the supporting 'evidence' has varied dramatically. For example, sometimes the President of the company is claimed to have been on the *Phil Donahue Show*; sometimes the *Jenny Jones Show*; sometimes the *Sally Jesse Raphael Show*. In fact, no senior executive of Procter & Gamble has ever appeared on any of these shows.[3] What is more, the allegation is obviously false, since neither the President nor the Board of a company such as Procter & Gamble has the right to allocate profits from the business to causes of their choice; the profits belong to the shareholders.

This story has been of particular interest to Christians. I have found it deeply perplexing to explain to Christian acquaintances who have been boycotting Procter & Gamble products for years that they have been hoaxed. To persuade them has been easier said than done in a world of spin and innuendo, where the norms of mass-media reporting care little for the time-honoured legal assumption, 'Innocent until proven guilty', preferring the pre-judgment, 'There's no smoke without fire.' In response to the question, 'Where's your evidence?', I have received the reply, 'Everyone knows it's true; it's all over the Internet.'

In response to this, a number of prominent leaders of Christian denominations and organizations have made public statements to the effect that the rumours about Procter & Gamble are false. For example, Victor B. Nelson, of the Billy Graham Evangelistic Association, stated: 'This rumor has been investigated. The conclusion reached by Christian leaders who are considered by Billy Graham to be reliable is that this rumor has no verifiable credibility.' Jerry Falwell, of Liberty University, said, 'These rumors need to be squelched. Many Christians and non-Christians alike are responsible for continuing to drag the name of Procter & Gamble through the mud and this should stop.' And the Right Reverend Herbert Thompson Jr, Bishop of Southern Ohio, explicitly articulates the burden of this chapter:

> The Episcopal Diocese of Southern Ohio has probably had more experience with the religious background of the founders and leaders of the Procter & Gamble Company than any other religious institution ... the Procter family ... [provided] buildings, land, and endowments that continue to sustain a vast number of the religious, social, and evangelical ministries of the Episcopal Church throughout Ohio and around the world ... Given our very close association with Procter

& Gamble for more than 150 years and our relationship with its people at every level, it is inconceivable that this absurd rumor about its trademark continues in circulation. Time after time these allegations have been shown to be utter fabrication, often spread viciously for personal gain. This is a misuse of religion and a violation of the Commandment against bearing false witness.[4]

Anonymous authority

What is so staggering about the tale of Procter & Gamble is the fact that claims of such seriousness, and such demonstrable vacuity, have survived and prospered for over twenty years. When we think of the impact of lies in our society, it is normal to dwell primarily on the role of the malicious or mistaken originator, and it's true that without an originator no lie will see the light of day. But in the case of the Procter & Gamble lie, the role of the originator is relatively minor by comparison with the ongoing contribution of thousands or even millions of people who accept it uncritically, nourish it, and keep it alive by passing it on.

Our generation's traditional means of mass communication – newspapers, books, broadcast media – are well established in our society, and so are the quality-control mechanisms around them. In the case of books, for instance, commissioning editors and their referees examine manuscripts to see whether they contain material good enough and fresh enough to publish. Copy-editors or others verify or, where necessary, correct factual information prior to publication. Eventually, the work is published under the author's name, and with the publisher clearly indicated. An author or publisher who gains a reputation for confusing invention with truth will soon lose credibility, and may face expensive lawsuits.

In contrast, anyone at all can sit down and in just a few minutes concoct a set of outrageous, slanderous claims about real people and publish them anonymously on the Internet. The rapid development of the Internet has made it hard for lawmakers to keep up. In many jurisdictions there is still no way for aggrieved parties to indict a slanderer if the slander is made anonymously in cyberspace. They don't even have a right to know the identity of the person making these claims against them.

This means that we must be wise in how we read what we find on the Internet. If we read claims, how can we know if they are true or not? In conventional publications, we might ask what the credentials of the author are, whether the publisher is reputable, whether reviews support or undermine the work, and so on. But when we read something that perplexes us in cyberspace, how can we weigh the authority of what we read? We can ask similar questions: 'Who is the author? Who runs the website or sends out the email? Has there been any critique of the material in other authoritative sources?' But in many cases, the work will be unsigned; or, if it is signed, we have no way of knowing whether it is a forgery or not. Unless it is a large organization with a profile in real space as well as cyberspace, the 'publisher' of the website may not be known to us, and may be unknowable except via the claims on the site. And most of the controversial content of the Internet goes undiscussed and unreviewed outside of cyberspace. Thus it can be extremely difficult to assess the authority of material found on the Web.

Have you ever been insulted by people who accuse Christians of being gullible? I have. And I find it sad, not so much because it's a barb aimed to hurt me, as because it shows that the speaker has not grasped that Christians should be *more* committed to the truth than anyone else. We believe in a personal Lord who *is* the Truth. When we share the gospel with our friends, we are asking them not to accept their current easy view of life just because everyone else does, but rather to open their eyes to the truth.

We must care not just about telling the truth ourselves, but about whether what we are told by others is true. In our listening and in our reading, we must be asking, 'How can I know whether this is true?' We can't assume that it is, and pass it on to others. In a wired world, unless we care enough to discriminate between substantiated fact and mere hearsay, we may easily find ourselves cast in the role of willing propagators of monstrous lies, as David Schenk observes:

> In the electronic age, a good lie well-told can zip around the world and back in a matter of seconds while the truth is trapped, buried under a filing cabinet full of statistics. While our fact-based society has largely overcome a past riddled with destructive myths and superstitions … one of the unwelcome consequences of information superabundance is that, in our increasingly distracted environment, we are more susceptible to simplifying, misleading myths.[5]

The apostle Paul wrote on a number of occasions about the danger to the early church of believing the popular myths in the surrounding culture (e.g. 1 Timothy 1:4; 4:7; 2 Timothy 4:4). Though the myths of our day may differ in content from those of Paul's, their basic characteristic remains the same: without evidence or support, they gain credibility only from being repeated often enough.

Malice aforethought

We live in a fallen world, in which fallen people sometimes lash out at others by fabricating untruths about them. The teaching of the Old Testament law takes account of this, and establishes standards for evidence in court cases. This affords some valuable principles for us:

> One witness is not enough to convict those accused of any crime or offence they may have committed. A matter must be established by the testimony of two or three witnesses.
>
> If a malicious witness takes the stand to accuse someone of a crime, the two involved in the dispute must stand in the presence of the LORD before the priests and the judges who are in office at the time. The judges must make a thorough investigation, and if the witness proves to be a liar, giving false testimony against another, then do to the false witness as that

witness intended to do to the other. You must purge
the evil from among you (Deuteronomy 19:15–19).

This principle of demanding a high standard of evidence
before believing an accusation against anyone was carried over
into the early church and applied, for example, in weighing
charges of misconduct against church elders (1 Timothy 5:19).
The Old Testament and the New agree that, in a fallen world, we
must defend the innocent against the false accusations of the
malicious. And we must take care not to become accomplices to
false witnesses by failing to test their claims adequately. The book
of Proverbs is full of teaching on the subject of truth and lies. It is
worth noting that it is not just the originators of the lies who are
judged, but also those who negligently believe them, finding it is
easier or more convenient to believe the lie than to hold out for
the truth.

Those who give false witness will perish,
and whoever listens to them will be destroyed for ever.
(Proverbs 21:28)

The Bible relates several examples of false witnesses who per-
verted the course of justice for malicious or self-serving ends. For
example, the martyr Stephen was set up by false witnesses, who
claimed: 'This fellow never stops speaking against this holy place
and against the law. For we have heard him say that this Jesus of
Nazareth will destroy this place and change the customs Moses
handed down to us' (Acts 6:13–14). The skewed and sensational-
ized account of the false witnesses whipped up the crowd to such
an extent that, as soon as Stephen said something they disagreed
with, it seemed to confirm their worst suspicions about him, and
they stoned him to death.

Death was also the outcome of the deliberate slandering of
Naboth, an inhabitant of Jezreel, where King Ahab had his
palace. Ahab fancied creating a new kitchen garden for the palace
in order to have a better supply of fresh vegetables, and the spot
that seemed best to him was exactly that occupied by Naboth's

vineyard. At first the king made him a reasonable offer: a better vineyard, or a handsome sum in cash. But this particular vineyard had been in Naboth's family for generations; he wasn't interested in selling. Ahab was not the most emotionally mature of Israel's kings, so he went home and shut himself in his bedroom in a fit of pique. His more gifted but famously devious wife Jezebel found him in a dark mood and persuaded him to explain what had happened.

'No problem!' she exclaimed, and wrote the following letter to the town councillors of Jezreel:

> Proclaim a day of fasting and seat Naboth in a prominent place among the people. But seat two scoundrels opposite him and have them testify that he has cursed both God and the king. Then take him out and stone him to death (1 Kings 21:9–10).

Events unfolded just as Jezebel had planned: Naboth was set up, cut down and buried. And Ahab got his beloved vegetable garden. What a travesty!

Jezebel's calculating malice may have been extreme, but it is not unique. It is possible to find Jezebels in every generation who are prepared to do any devilish thing to get what they want. And there are many more who will not think twice before telling a lie, even if it hurts someone else. So let's demand the highest standards of truth, and not become ignorant accomplices to malicious slanderers. 'For we are not unaware of [Satan's] schemes' (2 Corinthians 2:11).

Godless gossip

Perhaps we are scrupulous in checking out big news stories like the Procter & Gamble affair before we pass them on. But what about those tiny fragments of gossip about work colleagues, people in church, old acquaintances? Do we apply the same standards of truth to them?

There's something very satisfying about sharing a secret. The more scandalous the better! We love to whisper the hypocrisies of other people and point out the failings of those who seem 'perfect' in public.

The last few years can be seen as a remarkable renaissance for gossip, with the advent of email, instant messaging, chat rooms and SMS. Now gossip can carry on in a much wider circle, all day, every day, even in busy offices where the staff have their heads down apparently hard at work.

I once did business with a company from which I could not seem to get any results, until the management of the company did an audit of staff IT activities and discovered that my main point of contact was spending the majority of his time gossiping with friends on an instant messaging system.

Gossip can waste huge amounts of time. But this is not the main reason why the Bible has so much to say against it. The main reason is that gossip consists largely of talk about people in a manner that permits exaggeration and sensationalization. In this way it helps to maintain stereotypical judgments of individuals and keeps arguments on the boil. As Proverbs says,

> Without wood a fire goes out;
>> without gossip a quarrel dies down.
>>>>>>>> (Proverbs 26:20)

We say things about other people in gossip that we would never dream of saying to them face to face. As all these little snippets of conversation – the truths, half-truths, and downright lies – circulate and mix and cross-fertilize, misunderstandings and mistrusts build up, until discord results. It happens in schools and workplaces, in neighbourhoods and in churches; and, though each little piece of juicy gossip (what Proverbs 18:8 beautifully describes as 'choice morsels') seems harmless enough, the cumulative effect can be devastating for an individual on the receiving end of a whispering campaign of slander, or for whole communities reduced to dire dysfunctionality. If, somewhere in the mix, there is a person with an axe to grind or a chip on his or her shoulder, who doesn't just pass on gossip with the usual Chinese whispers, but who deliberately distorts the facts, then a truly horrible outcome can result. The apostle John writes in his last letter with great sadness about a church leader called Diotrophes, who keeps 'gossiping maliciously about us' (3 John 10) and thus poisoning the minds of his congregation against the apostle.

The church of Christ has no room for 'gossips and busybodies, saying things they ought not to' (1 Timothy 5:13). Rather, it is supposed to be a community of those who speak the truth in love (Ephesians 4:15).

Good words

For purveyors of godless gossip, for conspiracy theorists and for those who want to spin stories against others, new communications technologies must seem like a godsend. But if messages carried by the technology are false, misleading or slanderous, it is certainly not God's business that is being conducted. If the information superhighway becomes a trunk route for misinformation, something has gone terribly wrong: it has become a new lane on the broad road that leads to destruction (Matthew 7:13).

The Ninth Commandment warns us: 'You shall not give false testimony against your neighbour.' In fact, in the Old Testament law, it is not enough to avoid telling lies about your neighbour (by which the commandment means all with whom you come into contact), but you must also 'love your neighbour as yourself' (Leviticus 19:18).

If we love our neighbours, we shall not look for ways to hurt or lampoon them by falsely slandering them. Moreover, when they do genuinely do something wrong, we shall not turn their failures into a story to publicize for our own satisfaction. Rather, we shall seek their restoration as lovingly and privately as possible. This is what Jesus taught: 'If your brother or sister sins against you, go and show them their fault, just between the two of you. If they listen to you, you have won them over. But if they will not listen, take one or two others along, so that "every matter may be established by the testimony of two or three witnesses".' If they refuse to listen to them, tell it to the church …' (Matthew 18:15–17).

This is a long, long way from the flaming and public vilification one increasingly finds in cyberspace. The Jesus approach to relationships seeks the other person's welfare first, before our own. It is more interested in other people's honour than in our own. And it is rich in forgiveness; it does not have to have the last word.

If anyone has any right to say terrible things about others, it's surely Jesus. Our sins cost him his life. But, instead, he speaks peace to us and about us, and we can live because of it. So let's follow his example and bite our tongues when the desire rises in us to condemn others, to throw slander about or to gossip destructively. Let those who are without sin cast the first stone (John 8:7); I cannot. Let those who have no plank in their own eye point out the speck of sawdust in the eye of another (Luke 6:41–42); I cannot. We need to tame our tongues (James 3:1–12), and our typing fingers, so that our conversation (or chat or email or SMS) is 'always full of grace, seasoned with salt, so that [we may] know how to answer everyone' (Colossians 4:6). The requirements of the Ninth Net Commandment are simple, when we remember that Jesus could have called us 'enemies' but chose to call us 'friends' (Romans 5:10; John 15:14–15).

The Ninth Net Commandment

Do not slander anyone on the Internet.

Prayer

Lord, you know me and my words. I am a person of unclean lips. You know all the things I have said and written that have hurt others, and you. I know I should not have said these things.

[Confess any particular sins of speaking or slander that trouble your conscience.]

Please forgive me all these sins, and help me to communicate only what builds people up, whether in real space or in cyberspace. And may the words of my mouth and the meditation of my heart be pleasing in your sight, my Rock and my Redeemer.

In Jesus' name. Amen.

chapter 10
Enough is enough

You shall not covet your neighbour's house. You shall not
covet your neighbour's wife, or his male or female
servant, his ox or donkey, or anything that belongs to
your neighbour.
(Exodus 20:17)

It has been my privilege to visit several countries that are much
poorer than my own. I say it has been a privilege because I have
found that, in general, the fewer possessions people have, the
more generous they tend to be to friends and even to strangers
like me. It has almost made my heart burst when the poorest
people I have met have freely given me the best of what little they
have, although I have no real need of their gifts. Some of the gifts
I have counted most precious are worthless in financial terms,
but their value to me is beyond price because of what they signify.

This is what Jesus saw, when he was watching people deposit-
ing their offerings for the upkeep of the temple in Jerusalem. The
rich people paraded past with their big, fat charity donations. You
can almost hear the applause of the onlookers. And, no doubt,
the money would prove very useful to the temple managers. But
then a poor widow – someone with few means of survival in a

society with no welfare safety-net – came along and dropped two tiny copper coins into the collection plate. In our money, they were worth only a fraction of a penny. Jesus drew his disciples' attention to her action: 'I tell you the truth, this poor widow has put more into the treasury than all the others. They all gave out of their wealth; but she, out of her poverty, put in everything – all she had to live on' (Mark 12:43–44).

I recognize this woman: her heroic generosity, and her reckless determination to trust the Lord Jesus when he says: 'I tell you, do not worry about your life, what you will eat or drink; or about your body, what you will wear. Is not life more important than food, and the body more important than clothes? ... But seek first [God's] kingdom and his righteousness, and all these things will be given to you as well' (Matthew 6:25, 33).

I have met this woman, more than once, in some of the poor and forgotten places of our world, and I can testify that she is rich beyond the wealth of this world. But I have also met the heartless rich: those who will gladly donate respectable sums to charity so long as it is done under full spotlights at $1,000-a-plate charity fundraiser banquets[1]; people whose basic instincts are to grab and to hoard, not to give and to share.

Come to think of it, it isn't just the rich who fit into this category. It's most of us. Given a choice between 'more' and 'less', which of us can honestly say we'd rush to join the 'less' queue? That's not how we usually think. In theory, we agree that 'enough is enough'; we just don't have 'enough' yet.

There's a wonderful little verse tucked away towards the end of the book of Proverbs. It doesn't have much obvious connection with the verses around it; it just sits there, planting an unforgettable image in our minds:

> The leech has two daughters.
>   'Give! Give!' they cry.
>
>   (Proverbs 30:15)

Ugly creatures with insatiable appetites, that get fatter and fatter by sucking the life-blood of others: is that what we're like?

I didn't think so until the first time I returned home from a trip to a desperately poor country. Entering a well-stocked super-market, I was overwhelmed with a sense of shame and horror to be faced with such overabundance just a short aeroplane trip from the land I had so recently visited, where more and more parents are abandoning the babies they cannot feed, and where people are increasingly selling their own organs to wealthy west-erners because it is better to live with one kidney than to die with two.

When I look at the faces of the poor, it is easy to admit that they need more; but I am much more reluctant to admit that perhaps I also need less.

Hungry for more

'Less' is not a word often associated with the world of consumer electronics. Some years ago I participated in an official trade de-legation from Britain to Japan. My colleagues and I visited the headquarters of many of that country's electro-technical corpor-ate giants. The head-office meeting-rooms we visited were mostly furnished in cool, minimalist, almost ascetic, styles – a modern interpretation of traditional Zen design. The contrast between them and Akihabara could scarcely have been greater. Akihabara is Tokyo's 'Electric Town', and can reasonably be described as the gadget capital of the world. It consists of a bewildering concen-tration of neon-clad shops stuffed – yes, that is the best word – to the ceilings with a mind-numbing array of miniature electronic gizmos. 'The lights, like the myriad electronic products on offer, range from cool to gaudy, while the people, who seem incapable of standing still for very long, range from lightweight electro-nerd to hardcore technophile. The overall effect is equal parts exhilaration, delight, and exhaustion.'[2]

After an hour or two rummaging through this 'nerd's para-dise', I finally had to admit that there was nothing here I really needed. Yes, there were lots of ingenious inventions, and quite a few things that were beautiful to behold or amazingly miniatur-ized. But I really didn't need any of them.

This is not what's supposed to happen. As a well-behaved consumer – and a technophile, too – I'm not supposed to *need* a special reason to buy the latest gadget. The fact that it's new, that it's state of the art, or that it's going to be the Next Big Thing, should to be enough to part me from my cash. I'm supposed to need a good reason *not* to buy!

That's the theory that propels the whole high-technology business: keep inventing new gadgets or refining old ones to make them smaller, faster, more interconnected, or whatever, and consumers will keep buying, in some cases whether they need to or not.

Consider what's happened to the silicon chips that power modern computers. In 1965, Gordon Moore, the co-founder of Intel Corporation, predicted that the number of transistors that could be crammed on to a single chip would double every eighteen months for at least the next ten years.[3] In fact, this trend, which became known as 'Moore's Law', continued unabated for the next three-and-a-half decades, and still appears to be on track at the time of writing.

When I started out in computing, the amount of memory available in one of the computer systems I worked on was about the size of one of the many routine email messages I have received today. The first personal computer I owned had 256Kb of RAM (that's about 265,000 bytes) and the hard disk had 18Mb (that's 18 million bytes). I thought that amazingly highly specified at the time. The PC I most recently bought has 1Gb of RAM (a gigabyte is about 1,000 million bytes) and 6Gb on the hard disk. It's not uncommon to find myself using computers with terabytes of storage (a terabyte is approximately a million million bytes).

Twenty years ago, the programs we wrote were always short of memory, and their lack of processing power made them limp along. If only we had just a few more resources, we thought, everything would run like an express train. Now, we have more resources than we could ever have imagined back then, yet our programs still need *just a little more* to run *really* well. Our expectations and aspirations have grown so that we always write resource-hungry programs that need just a little bit more than we can have, even today. Never mind: Moore's Law will come to our rescue with extra cheap power to make our programs run, and the continuing growth in memory size and the drop in memory price will help bail us out. But by the time the next cycle of Moore's Law turns, of course, we shall have moved on to bigger projects, with greater demands that will still outstrip the available resources.

Ironically, in our hunger for more power and *memory*, we quickly *forget* the target we were aiming for, as we forever redefine our goals to be one step ahead of the advance of techno-logical capabilities. It's not our programs that have become greedy for resources – it's us.

The challenge to aim for 'enough' rather than constantly striv-ing for 'more' goes far beyond specialist programmers who worry about getting their hands on a few extra bytes. It concerns every-one who uses technology and who is tempted by the allure of shiny new high-tech equipment.

According to Agur, the son of Jakeh, who wrote part of the book of Proverbs (including the unforgettable image of the leech's two daughters):

> There are three things that are never satisfied,
>   four that never say, 'Enough!':
> the grave, the barren womb,
>   land, which is never satisfied with water,
>   and fire, which never says, 'Enough!'
>
> (Proverbs 30:15–16)

What might he have written if he had lived in our culture? I wonder if consumers would have featured in his list.

> There are three consumers who are never satisfied,
>   four who never say 'Enough!':
> followers of fashion, DIY enthusiasts,
>   programmers, who are never satisfied with the
>   resources they have,
>   and gadget geeks, who never say, 'Enough!'

Many of us are sitting targets for the marketing executives who keep throwing buzzwords and phrases at us: 'new', 'next-generation', 'leading-edge', 'state-of-the-art', 'upgrade', 'enhanced functionality', 'improved communications', 'portable', 'wireless', 'miniature' … We lose touch with *what* the technology does, and *why* we thought we needed it in the first place, and instead base our purchasing decisions on *how* it does what it does and *who* else has got it.

Suppose I like to listen to music from time to time. I've got a cassette player and a good supply of cassettes, so that ought to do the job. Well, yes, but the sound quality can be a bit dodgy, especially as the tapes get older. What I really need is a CD player. OK, so I buy a CD player, and then I have to replace my cassette music collection with CDs. Now I can relax, can't I? No, not yet. I can progress to DVDs. They can give me lots of additional information and perhaps some video footage too. Sooner or later, CDs are bound to become obsolete, so I might as well start buying DVDs now and avoid the expense of replacing my CD library. But hang on, why build up a bulky, dust-gathering library of music at all? Why not use the Internet as a virtual library, and download just the tracks I really want into an MP3 player?

And so the rationale for technology upgrades or replacements runs on and on, ever more tied up with the detail of techno-fashion and an attempt to second-guess the future. Where is the original requirement in all this? I wanted to listen to some music from time to time. On reflection, perhaps a basic radio would have been perfectly adequate.

The same challenges face us in every area of technology. The average lifespan of a PC in business is three years or less, not because the machines stop working, but because we stop being satisfied with what they offer. It must be admitted, though, that the strategies of the leading suppliers in the IT industry drive this forward relentlessly. Major software companies release substantially altered versions of their products on short cycles of one or two years, and as soon as they can get away with it they stop supporting the second-to-last release, so consumers *have to* upgrade or risk being left behind with an irreparable system.

There are difficult choices to be made. How often do we properly examine the issues? The Roman writer Ovid wrote, 'Plenty makes me poor.'[4] One way in which our plenty, our comparative wealth, impoverishes us is that often it encourages us not to consider whether we really need something at all; instead, we just go ahead and get it anyway.

Building bigger systems

We live in a materialistic age, but we do not have a materialistic Lord. When Jesus sent out the seventy-two trainee evangelists, he told them not to take a lot of luggage with them (Luke 10:1–4). According to Jesus, material wealth can be a spiritual snare, lulling us into a comfortable lifestyle in which we can rely more on our riches on earth than we do on our Father in heaven (Luke 6:24). It's not impossible for rich people to be Christians; it's just very, very hard (Matthew 19:23–26). The problem is not the riches themselves, but the hold they have on our hearts. Either Jesus is our Lord, or we have no place with him. That means he will always, sooner or later, challenge his rivals in our lives. People place their trust in their money, so the Lord lays it down in black and white: 'You cannot be a slave to both God and Money' (Matthew 6:24).

When a rich young man came to Jesus asking how he might inherit eternal life, Jesus first pointed him in the direction of obedience to God's law. When the man maintained that he followed the law religiously, Jesus shifted the challenge from his head to his heart by going for his wallet.

> Jesus answered, 'If you want to be perfect, go, sell your possessions and give to the poor, and you will have treasure in heaven. Then come, follow me.'
> When the young man heard this, he went away sad, because he had great wealth (Matthew 19:21–22).

Jesus' challenge found the young man out. He thought he could say, 'I'm yours, Lord, but my money's my own', but that's not an option Jesus will permit. If we turn our money over to the

Lord, he may allow us to manage it as his stewards; but it must be his, not ours, to decide, and we may neither horde it like the man who buried his talent in the ground (Matthew 25:14–30) nor squander it like the prodigal son (Luke 15:11–32).

The Tenth Commandment warns: 'You shall not covet your neighbour's house. You shall not covet your neighbour's wife, or his male or female servant, his ox or donkey, or anything that belongs to your neighbour.' Coveting is not stealing. It's not helping yourself. It's just gazing over the fence at your neighbour's belongings and thinking, 'I've really got to get my hands on one like that.' It's letting the thought fester inside until it results either in bitterness (if it remains unfulfilled) or self-indulgence (if it is fulfilled through acquiring the object of desire).

Notice that the commandment leaves open the question of why these things are desirable. Perhaps the fact that they are owned by the neighbour plays a part: 'Why should he have the super-de-luxe model, when I've only got the standard edition?'

Much of the consumerism of our society is driven by covetousness. Manufacturers show us their wares and ask, 'Wouldn't you like to have one of these?' And then they show us rich, famous, glamorous celebrities with the same wares, and say, 'Have you seen who's got one? You'll need to get a move on and buy one too if you want to keep your credibility.'

The age-old human sin of covetousness used to be known as 'keeping up with the Joneses'. Now, at least in the context of technology, it's called 'keeping up to date' (where this is not related to actual need, but rather to some socially accepted standard of 'coolness'). I suspect that trying to keep your system 'so hot it's cool' leaves Jesus cold.

Jesus told a parable about the system-upgrade strategy of a wealthy entrepreneur. His fields produced such a good crop that he thought it would ensure his permanent peace of mind and material security. His storage barns were not big enough to store all the grain, so he tore the barns down and upgraded them to larger models. Then he stored his grain and all his prized possessions in the new barns. Now he would enjoy his life of self-indulgence.

'But God said to him, "You fool! This very night your life will be demanded from you. Then who will get what you have prepared for yourself?"

'This is how it will be with those who store up things for themselves but are not rich towards God' (Luke 12:20–21).

The old yuppie bumper sticker reads: 'Life's a game: whoever dies with the most toys wins.' This is diametrically opposite to the truth, as the parable of the rich man and Lazarus makes painfully clear (Luke 16:19–31). Jesus encourages us to invest in heaven, where interest accrues for eternity, not in the short-term, high-risk 'toys' of this world:

'Do not store up for yourselves treasures on earth, where moth and rust destroy, and where thieves break in and steal. But store up for yourselves treasures in heaven, where moth and rust do not destroy, and where thieves do not break in and steal. For where your treasure is, there your heart will be also' (Matthew 6:19–21).

We shall all stand before the Lord to give an account of ourselves. We can be sure that on that day the raw processing power of our computer, or the fashionability of its make, or the number of peripheral devices attached, will not impress the Lord nearly as much as it impressed us in this life. What *will* impress him is the openness of our heart to him, and the extent to which we have learned to find contentment in him rather than in the time-bound consumer durables around us.

Paul proved in his own life the possibility of living in contentment, independently of material circumstances, and we can prove it in ours too. He wrote: 'I know what it is to be in need, and I know what it is to have plenty. I have learned the secret of being content in any and every situation, whether well fed or hungry, whether living in plenty or in want. I can do everything through him who gives me strength' (Philippians 4:12–13).

It is not that having some great computer kit is fundamentally wrong. Rather it is – or should be – completely irrelevant to our personal happiness. The Lord didn't call us to build a great system configuration; he called us to build his kingdom. And he didn't call us to wish our lives away, drooling over the latest gear; he called us to devote our lives to him and to find peace in his loving care. That's why the Tenth Net Commandment is so important:

The Tenth Net Commandment

Do not upgrade your computer system beyond what
you reasonably need.

We need to be on our guard against all kinds of greed; life does not consist in the abundance of our possessions (Luke 12:15). As G. K. Chesterton wrote, 'There are two ways to get enough. One is to accumulate more. The other is to need less.' When we learn to desire the toys of this world less and less, and begin to rely absolutely on the Lord of all, we find perfect contentment in him (see 1 Timothy 6:6–8).

Prayer

Lord, you are the creator of all good things. Forgive me when I value mere created things more highly than I value you. Forgive me when I fall into unhealthy patterns of thought about things I'd like to have. Forgive me when I covet what other people have.

[Confess any specific sins of covetousness or materialism.]

Please forgive me my sins and create in me a clean heart. Protect me in my thought life from the attractions of mere things. Please help me to find my contentment in you and to please you in the way I think about and use technology. And please give me practical wisdom to recognize when I have enough, and courage to act on that knowledge.

In Jesus' name. Amen.

Conclusion

We have thought through some of the demands of the age-old
Ten Commandments of the Bible for us in this age of high technology. We have explored whether a moral code originally given
in the lowest of low technologies – roughly chiselled stones –
could have anything at all to say to us as we sit in front of our
state-of-the-art computers. More specifically, through an understanding of these biblical commands we have tried to find help in
the moral choices we make as users of information technology.

Our investigation has led to some clear conclusions. The first
is that the moral requirements of an eternal God don't have an
expiry date. The psalmist tells us:

> Your word, O LORD, is eternal;
> it stands firm in the heavens.
> Your laws endure to this day,
> for all things serve you.

> (Psalm 119:89, 91)

We cannot credibly argue that rules carved in stone have no
relevance for actions carried out in silicon. God's moral requirements are defined, not by fashion or whim, but by his own
unchanging character.

Secondly, nothing in all the world lies beyond the scope of God's law, or of his grace.

> Where can I go from your Spirit?
>   Where can I flee from your presence?
> If I go up to the heavens, you are there;
>   if I make my bed in the depths, you are there.
> If I rise on the wings of the dawn,
>   if I settle on the far side of the sea,
> even there your hand will guide me,
>   your right hand will hold me fast.
>
> (Psalm 139:7–10)

God knows much more about new technology than we do. He knows its strengths and weaknesses, its opportunities and threats for us. When we pick up a new gadget, he's there waiting for us, longing for us to honour him in the way we use it, eager that we should remember him in every new situation we face. This world doesn't have any no-go zones for God, and cyberspace is no exception. Either we decide to follow him through *all* of life or we are not really following him at all.

Thirdly, we must not live by mere instincts, responding like animals to every new challenge life throws in our way. The Lord calls us to meditate on his Word, so that the mind of Christ may be formed in us, so we can live to please him. We should not merely *live*; we should decide ahead of time how to *live to please God*, and then do so! Following a holy God in an impure world will always involve some challenges and persecution. Unless we get used to putting God first when times are easy, it is unlikely that we shall put him first when the going gets tough.

Fourthly, living to please God is not just about what we believe. It is about practical action – what we do when we sit at the computer keyboard. James reminds us that 'faith by itself, if it is not accompanied by action, is dead' (James 2:17).

Fifthly, practical action is not enough by itself; it must flow from a living faith in God. Many people have tried to codify principles for 'good citizenship' with new technology. For example, Virginia Shea has defined the following set of 'Core Rules of Netiquette' (how to behave towards others on the Internet):

1. Remember the human.
2. Adhere to the same standards of behaviour online that you follow in real life.
3. Know where you are in cyberspace.
4. Respect other people's time and bandwidth.
5. Make yourself look good online.
6. Share expert knowledge.
7. Help keep flame wars under control.
8. Respect other people's privacy.
9. Don't abuse your power.
10. Be forgiving of other people's mistakes.[1]

These are excellent suggestions for good conduct online, and I commend them to readers to consider – with some reservations about number 5. As a Christian I believe that we humans have a profound problem with being truly and consistently good. The only way we will be able to behave with purity in the long run is to stop *trying to be good by keeping rules*, and instead devote ourselves to *loving the Lord our God with all our heart and with all our soul and with all our strength* (Deuteronomy 6:5). Notice that we are to love God with all our 'strength' as well as with all our heart and soul. Love for God is more than a warm feeling inside; it overflows into outward action. In fact, love for God may lead us to do things we don't feel like doing, or not to do things we do feel like doing. For the sake of our beloved Lord we do what pleases him, not what pleases us. True love is never passive; it is the most powerful force for action in the universe.

This leads us to our sixth conclusion: that we shall not win God's love simply by putting the Net Commandments into practice. In fact, if our focus is on obeying the rules, we shall not succeed in putting them into practice at all. But if we grasp the miraculous truth that he loved us so much *already* that he offered his only Son as a substitute for us on the cross, and if we love him in return above all else, he will bless our attempts to please him in what we do, however faltering they may be. The Net Commandments will not open the doors of heaven to us, but they will help us to say, 'Thank you, Lord, for adopting me as your child.'

Finally, if you approach the end of this book feeling thoroughly depressed because you have come to realize how often you let God down, don't despair. The Lord Jesus knew what you were like before he died for you, but he still chose to go through with it. Why? Because someone had to pay the price for your sin, and Jesus freely volunteered. Now he comes with forgiveness as his gift to those who will cast themselves on God's mercy. John assures us that 'If we confess our sins, he is faithful and just and will forgive us our sins and purify us from all unrighteousness' (1 John 1:9).

Let us grasp and hold on to the fact that Jesus loves us so much more than we allow ourselves to believe. Because of our small view of his love for us, we tend to love him much less than we should. Remember when Peter committed the dreadful treachery of denying that he even knew who Jesus was? Did Jesus disown him? Amazingly, no. Well, did Jesus give him a lecture about how he should always tell the truth, do the right thing and stand up for his faith? No. Jesus simply asked him three questions, one for each of Peter's denials: 'Simon, son of John, do you truly love me more than these?' … 'Simon, son of John, do you truly love me?' … 'Simon, son of John, do you love me?' (John 21:15, 16, 17).

Love is the key. Our goodness and holiness must flow out of our love for Jesus, and our love for him is possible only because he first loved us.

So do you truly love him?

It was an older, wiser Peter, a man who had learned in his heart to 'set apart Christ as Lord' (1 Peter 3:15), who brought us this encouragement, which speaks loudly to us of love's response: 'As obedient children, do not conform to the evil desires you had when you lived in ignorance. But just as he who called you is holy, so be holy in all you do' (1 Peter 1:14–15).

My prayer is that this book will help and encourage you to be holy as you live for Christ in a rapidly changing world of new technology, and that in serving the Lord you will find great joy.

Prayer

Lord, thank you for loving me. Please fill me with your love, so that my whole life may express thanksgiving and praise to you. Help me to love you with all my heart and soul and strength, and help me to love my neighbour as myself.

Lord, I long to be holy even as you are holy. Please fill me with your Holy Spirit to strengthen and guide me in your ways. Help me to walk in paths of righteousness whatever I do in life, so that I may bring joy to your heart.

Dear Lord, I offer my prayer to you in Jesus' precious name. Amen.

The Net Commandments

1. Put God first in cyberspace.
2. Do not allow technology to become an idol.
3. Do not say anything in cyberspace that misrepresents God or his gospel.
4. Do not get into addictive patterns of computer use: set aside regular off-line time that is sacred to God and non-negotiable.
5. Do not use your knowledge of new technology to humiliate the older generation.
6. Do not play with violence or act irresponsibly towards others in cyberspace.
7. Do not have anything to do with pornography, perversion or inappropriate relationships on the Internet.
8. Do not steal electronic money or information, or violate software copyright.
9. Do not slander anyone on the Internet.
10. Do not upgrade your computer system beyond what you reasonably need.

Notes

Preface

1. Warren, Loschin, and Montez received lengthy custodial sentences. 'Jane' is a pseudonym.

Introduction

1. Third edition, 1995.
2. Douglas Coupland, *Microserfs* (London: Flamingo, 1995), p. 357.
3. For a finely nuanced Christian reading of the times, see theologian David F. Wells's magnificent trilogy (published by IVP, Leicester): *No Place for Truth* (1993), *God in the Wasteland* (1994), and *Losing our Virtue* (1998).
4. For example, C. S. Lewis, *Mere Christianity* (London: Fontana, 1952); C. Steven Evans, *Why Believe?* (Leicester: IVP, 1996); Vaughan Roberts, *Turning Points* (Carlisle: Paternoster, 1999).

1. God first

1. There have been many Christian explorations of the Ten Commandments. Recent examples include Stuart Briscoe, *The Ten Commandments: Playing by the Rules* (Carlisle: OM, 1993); J. John, *Ten* (Eastbourne: Kingsway, 2000); David Field, *God's Good Life: The Ten Commandments for the 21st Century* (Leicester: IVP, 1992).
2. Third edition, 1995.

2. God only

1. L. Ryken, J. C. Wilhoit and T. Longman III (eds.), *Dictionary of Biblical Imagery* (Leicester: IVP, 1998), p. 418.
2. J. A. Motyer, in I. H. Marshall, A. R. Millard, J. I. Packer and D. J. Wiseman (eds.), *New Bible Dictionary*, 3rd ed. (Leicester: IVP, 1996), p. 496.
3. 'The Green Eye of the Yellow God', by J. Milton Hayes (1911).
4. Bob Goudzwaard, *Idols of Our Time* (Downers Grove, IL: IVP, 1981), p. 13.
5. Ibid., pp. 21–22.
6. Ibid., p. 22.
7. Neil Postman, *Technopoly: The Surrender of Culture to Technology* (New York: Vintage, 1992), p. 5.
8. Neil Postman, *The End of Education: Redefining the Value of School* (New York: Knopf, 1995), p. 38.
9. From the editor's introduction in S. Monsma (ed.), *Responsible Technology* (Grand Rapids, MI: Eerdmans, 1986), pp. 49–50.
10. Robert Jastrow, *The Enchanted Loom* (New York: Simon & Schuster, 1981), p. 162.
11. Douglas R. Groothuis, *Unmasking the New Age* and *Confronting the New Age* (both Leicester: IVP, 1986).
12. Douglas R. Groothuis, *The Soul in Cyberspace* (Grand Rapids, MI: Baker, 1997), pp. 109, 110.
13. Bart Kosko, 'Heaven in a chip', *Datamation*, 1995.
14. Ibid.
15. Ryken, Wilhoit and Longman III (eds.), *Dictionary of Biblical Imagery*, pp. 336–337.
16. This is reflected in the title of Jim Jubak's book *In the Image of the Brain: Breaking the Barrier Between the Human Mind and Intelligent Machines* (Boston, MA: Little, Brown, 1992).
17. Westminster Shorter Catechism, Answer I (1647).
18. The relationship between God and his people is frequently illustrated in terms of marriage in the Bible. See, for example, Hosea 1 – 3, Ephesians 5:22 – 33; Revelation 19:9; 21:1–2.

3. God's name

1. *Mercedes Benz* by Janis Joplin and Bob Newirth (Columbia Records, 1971).
2. Paul Weston, *Why We Can't Believe* (Leicester: Frameworks, 1991), p. 56.

4. Sacred to God

1. Kimberly S. Young, *Caught in the Net* (Wiley: Chichester, 1998), pp. 35–36.

2. *The Times Higher Education Supplement*, 10 January 1997, p. 29.
3. *AST IT Barometer Survey*, Autumn 1996, p. 7.
4. *Metro*, 11 May 2001, p. 7.
5. Young, *Caught in the Net*, pp. 3–5. To take Dr Young's Net addiction test online visit www.netaddiction.com.
6. Ibid., p. 123.
7. Ibid., p. 46.

5. The generation gap

1. Queen Victoria, letter to the Crown Princess of Prussia, 5 January 1876.
2. Oscar Wilde, *A Woman of No Importance* (1893).
3. Cyril Connolly, Tom Driberg speech in House of Commons, 30 October 1959.
4. Mark Twain (attributed in *Reader's Digest*, September 1939, but not traced in his written works).
5. Don Tapscott, *Growing Up Digital: The Rise of the Net Generation* (McGraw-Hill: London, 1998), p. 36.
6. Phrase coined by Apple Computer visionary Alan Kay.
7. Seymour Papert, *The Connected Family* (Atlanta, GA: Longstreet, 1996), p. 30.
8. 'Nerve-wracking demo news from US State Department', *Washington Post*, 20 February 1997.
9. Tapscott, *Growing Up Digital*, p. 37.
10. To misappropriate Sir Winston Churchill's memorable phrase.
11. Tapscott, *Growing Up Digital*, p. 49.
12. C. G. Jung, 'The Development of Personality', in *Collected Works* 17 (Princeton, NJ: Princeton University Press, 1934), p. 284.
13. Quoted in Tapscott, *Growing Up Digital*, pp. 36–37.
14. Ibid.
15. Ibid.
16. Ibid., p. 38.

6. Death to hacking

1. For more on this delightful topic, see Brian Leibowitz, *The Journal of the Institute for Hacks, TomFoolery, and Pranks at MIT* (Cambridge, MA: MIT Museum, 1982); Ira Haverson and Tiffany Fulton-Pearson, *Is This the Way to Baker House? A Compendium of MIT Hacking Lore* (Cambridge, MA: MIT Museum, 1982); and my personal favourite, Neil Steinberg, *If At All Possible, Involve a Cow* (New York: St Martin's, 1992).
2. From the *IHTFP Hack Gallery*, http://hacks.mit.edu/Hacks/misc/ethics.html.

3. Sherry Turkle, *Life On Screen: Identity in the Age of the Internet* (London: Weidenfeld & Nicolson, 1995), pp. 31–32.

4. In MIT jargon, such people are known as 'crackers'.

5. Part of a computer network designed to keep intruders out.

6. *Panorama*, BBC1, 3 July 2000.

7. Derived from the Monty Python comedy sketch in which diners are informed that the menu includes 'egg and bacon; egg, sausage and bacon; egg and Spam; egg, bacon and Spam; egg, bacon, sausage and Spam; Spam, bacon, sausage and Spam; Spam, egg, Spam; Spam, bacon and Spam;' etc.

8. David Shenk, *Data Smog: Surviving the Information Glut* (London: Abacus, 1997), p. 25.

9. Laurence A. Canter and Martha S. Siegel, *How to Make a Fortune on the Information Superhighway* (London: HarperCollins, 1995).

10. Douglas Coupland, *Microserfs* (London: Flamingo, 1995), p. 357.

11. Robert Uhlig, 'Virus jokers risk global shutdown', *The Daily Telegraph*, 3 April 1999, p. 19.

12. David Grossman, 'Trained to kill', *Christianity Today*, August 1998, p. 36.

13. Quoted in Jody Veenker, 'Moral combat', *Christianity Today*, March 2000.

14. 'Children are harmed by video games', *Metro*, 20 August 2001, p. 7.

15. Quoted in Veenker, 'Moral combat'.

16. David Grossman, 'Trained to kill', p. 36.

7. Let's talk about sex

1. 'We've got porn', *Christianity Today*, June 2000.

2. Don Tapscott, *Growing Up Digital: The Rise of the Net Generation* (London: McGraw-Hill, 1998), p. 238.

3. Ibid., p. 239.

4. John Houghton, 'Pornucopia', *Renewal* 287 (2000), p. 43.

5. Nicholas Thompson, *The Washington Monthly*, July/August 2000, p. 27.

6. Ibid., p. 30.

7. *Church Times*, 14 January 2000, p. 2.

8. Nicholas Thompson, *The Washington Monthly*, July/August 2000, pp. 27–28.

9. Ibid., p. 31.

8. Give and take

1. 'Are ATMs easy targets for crooks?' *Chicago Tribune*, 15 August 1986; *Business Week*, 6 March 1989.

2. *Software Engineering Notes* 13.3, July 1988.

3. *Financial Times*, 2 September 1986.
4. Keith Hearnden, 'Computer criminals are human too', in Tom Forester (ed.), *Computers in the Human Context* (Oxford: Basil Blackwell, 1989), p. 420.
5. Leslie D. Ball, 'Computer crime', in Tom Forester (ed.), *The Information Technology Revolution* (Oxford: Basil Blackwell, 1985), p. 536.
6. Hugo Cornwall, *Datatheft: Computer Fraud, Industrial Espionage and Information Crime* (London: Heinemann, 1987).
7. *Computer Talk*, 11 March 1991.
8. Tom Forester and Perry Morrison, *Computer Ethics: Cautionary Tales and Ethical Dilemmas in Computing*, 2nd ed. (Cambridge, MA: MIT Press, 1994).
9. Ibid., p. 30.

9. Reputations

1. Amway Corporation has consistently maintained that it 'does not condone the spreading of false and malicious rumors against Procter & Gamble'.
2. www.pg.com/about_pg/overview_facts/trademark_facts.jhtml.
3. Copies of letters confirming this from the producers of the TV shows can be inspected on the Procter & Gamble website, www.pg.com.
4. Copies of these and other original letters of support from prominent Christians can be found on the Procter & Gamble website.
5. David Schenk, *Data Smog: Surviving the Information Glut* (London: Abacus, 1997), p. 156.

10. Enough is enough

1. Mark 6:1–4 offers God's perspective on public charity.
2. Daniel Skuka, 'Akihabara' (2000), www.japaninc.net/mag/comp/2000/11/nov00_guide.html.
3. Gordon E. Moore, 'Cramming more components onto integrated circuits', *Electronics*, April 1965.
4. Ovid (Publius Ovidus Naso, 43 BC – AD 17) *Metamorphoses*, 3: *'Inopem me copia fecit.'*

Conclusion

1. Virginia Shea, *Netiquette* (San Rafael: Albion Books, 1994), ch. 3.